Fear Street

Ice-Cold Terror –
He's coming to get you

von R. L. Stine

PONS GmbH
Stuttgart

PONS

Fear Street
Ice-Cold Terror – He's coming to get you

von R. L. Stine

Originaltitel:
Fear Street – Haunted

Auflage A1 ⁴ ³ ² ¹ / 2015 2014 2013 2012

© PONS GmbH, Rotebühlstraße 77, 70178 Stuttgart, 2012
PONS Produktinfos und Shop: www.pons.de
PONS Sprachenportal: www.pons.eu
E-Mail: info@pons.de
Alle Rechte vorbehalten.

Redaktion: Canan Eulenberger-Özdamar
Englische Überarbeitung, Annotationen und Übungen: Brian Melican
Korrektorat: Brian Wolfe
Logoentwurf: Erwin Poell, Heidelberg
Logoüberarbeitung: Sabine Redlin, Ludwigsburg
Einbandgestaltung: Daniel Müller, Stuttgart
Coverillustration: Silvia Christoph, aus R.L. Stine Fear Street – Eiskalter Hass,
© für die deutsche Ausgabe 2009 Loewe Verlag GmbH Bindlach
Tonaufnahmen/Digital Mastering: allegria Musik-/Audioproduktion GbR
Sprecher: Brian Munatones
Layout: Digraf.pl – dtp services
Satz: Satz und mehr, Besigheim
Druck und Bindung: L.E.G.O. S.p.A., Lavis (TN)

Printed in Italy.
ISBN: 978-3-12-010075-1

INHALTSANGABE

„Ich bin nicht verrückt", denkt Melissa. Doch sie ist die Einzige, die den Einbrecher sehen kann. Und der macht ihr das Leben zur Hölle: Er manipuliert ihre Bremsen und stößt sie beinahe aus dem Fenster. Wer ist er? Und was will er von ihr? Melissa weiß nur eins: Sie muss ganz schnell sein Geheimnis lüften – bevor sie tot ist!

AUFTRETENDE PERSONEN

Melissa
Melissa wohnt in der Fear Street und wird von einem unheimlichen Geist heimgesucht.

Buddy
Buddy ist Melissas Freund und macht sich Sorgen um sie. Er glaubt nicht an Geister und denkt, dass Melissa psychologische Hilfe braucht.

Paul
Paul erscheint Melissa - und nur Melissa. Andere Menschen können ihn nicht sehen oder hören.

Beantworte die Fragen, die in den Kapiteln auftauchen und sich mit wichtigen Punkten der Geschichte beschäftigen. Die Lösungen dazu findest du ab S. 122.

R.L. Stine

CHAPTER 1

Melissa Dryden sat up[1] in bed and screamed[2].
Still half asleep, she felt the fear fall over her like a suffocating[3] blanket.
She screamed again as the noise at the bedroom window got louder. "No–
please! Don't come in here!"
She tried to get out of bed, but her legs were caught[4] in the bed sheet.
Breathing hard, trying to hold back her panic, she pulled herself free and
stumbled[5] toward the door–just as her father burst in[6].
"Lissa–what is it?"
She ran to him and pointed to the window. "Someone is out there," she
said. The noise at the window grew louder.
"Huh?" He looked at the window, heard the noise. Melissa tried to stop him,
but he hurried toward the window. "No, Dad, wait–" He was always so
reckless[7]. She wanted to run from the room. But she couldn't leave her dad.
Why was he laughing?
"Come here, Lissa."
"What is it?" She took a few hesitant[8] steps toward the window. Mr.
Dryden, smiling and shaking his head, held back the curtain and pointed
outside. "Here's your prowler.[9]"
"It's a tree branch[10], right?"
"Right."
"What on earth is going on?" Melissa's mother came hurrying into the room
and turned on the lamp.
"Nothing to be concerned about," Mr. Dryden said, looking out at the sky.
"Full moon[11]. Look at that. The moon's always so big in August."

---

1 **to sit up** – *sich aufrichten*
2 **to scream** – *schreien*
3 **suffocating** – *erstickend*
4 **caught** – *gefangen*
5 **to stumble** – *stolpern*
6 **to burst in** – *hereinplatzen*
7 **reckless** – *waghalsig, unbesonnen*
8 **hesitant** – *zögerlich*
9 **prowler** – *Spanner, Eindringling, Einbrecher*
10 **branch** – *Ast*
11 **full moon** – *Vollmond*

"I don't want to hear about the moon. I want to know what all the screaming was about," Mrs. Dryden said sharply[1].

"Lissa heard a tree tapping at her window."

"A tree?"

"I thought it was a burglar[2]," she said, falling back onto the bed. "The noise woke me up and—"

"You shouldn't watch the news before you go to bed," Mrs. Dryden said. She walked over and squeezed[3] Melissa's hand. "All the talk about that prowler—"

"Well, there is a Fear Street Prowler, Mother. I didn't imagine that, you know. Someone has been breaking into houses on Fear Street and—"

"We've lived on Fear Street for five years without any problems," her mother said, pushing Melissa's blonde hair back off her forehead[4]. "Don't you ever brush your hair?"

"I like it wild. Anyways, sorry," Melissa said. "I'm okay. We can go back to bed now."

"What time did you get in tonight?" Mrs. Dryden asked. "Late, I'll bet[5]."

"Yeah. It was pretty[6] late. I'm not sure when."

"Pretty late or very late?"

"Come on, Mom," Melissa said, sitting up. "Summer's over in a week. Buddy and I haven't had a chance to see each other. He was on vacation with his parents for two weeks and—"

"Well, that's why you're screaming your head off, imagining prowlers. You're overtired[7]."

Melissa groaned[8]. That was her mother's explanation for everything. If you messed up[9] on a test, or didn't feel like eating, or were in a bad mood, it was because you were overtired.

---

1 **sharp** – (hier:) bissig, scharf
2 **burglar** – Einbrecher
3 **to squeeze sb.'s hand** – jdm. die Hand fest drücken
4 **forehead** – Stirn
5 **..., I'll bet** – ..., nicht wahr?
6 **pretty** – (ugs.) ziemlich
7 **overtired** – übermüdet
8 **to groan** – ächzen
9 **to mess up** – vergeigen

"Mother, for the last time, there really is a prowler on Fear Street. It's in the newspaper practically[1] every day."

"It's so hot in here," her mother said. She never could stick to a subject[2]. "It's eighty degrees[3] outside. Why don't you open that window?"

"I–I really don't want to," Melissa said, feeling a little of the fear creep back.

"Well then, let's go to bed. Are you coming, Wes?" She pulled her husband's sleeve.

"Yeah. Sure. But come here a minute, Lissa. I want to show you something."

"Huh? Can't it wait till morning?" Melissa suddenly felt very sleepy.

"No. Come on." He grabbed both of her hands and pulled her easily out of bed. "Wow, you're so light."

"Are you going on again about how skinny[4] I am?"

"No. Come on. I want to show you something that will make you feel better." His expression grew serious as he pulled her across the hall to their bedroom.

"Wes, really–let her get some sleep. She's very overtired," her mother said, following behind.

"This'll only take a second. I want to calm her down," Mr. Dryden said, clicking on the ceiling light. They stepped into the large bedroom, which always smelled of Mrs. Dryden's perfume. Melissa's father pulled her to his bed table and then let go of her hands. He pulled the drawer of the bed table out and reached right into the back of the drawer. "Here it is," he said, with a grim[5] smile on his round face.

He held up a small silver pistol.

Melissa's mouth dropped open. "A gun? Is it real?"

Mr. Dryden dropped it into her hand. It felt much heavier than it looked and was cold to the touch. "Of course it's real. And it's loaded[6]." Melissa shuddered[7] and quickly handed the gun back to him.

---

1 **practically** – *(hier:) so gut wie*
2 **to stick to a subject** – *bei einem Thema bleiben*
3 **degrees** – *Grad (hier: Grad Fahrenheit (US-amerikanische Maßeinheit) 80 Grad Fahrenheit = 26,6 Grad Celsius)*
4 **skinny** – *dünn, mager*
5 **grim** – *düster, betrüblich*
6 **loaded** – *geladen*
7 **to shudder** – *erschaudern*

"Hey, don't look so terrified. I've been hunting since I was ten. I know a lot about guns."

"Put it away, Wes," Mrs. Dryden said from the other side of the bed. She yawned[1] loudly.

"I bought it just after I read the first news story about the Fear Street Prowler. I just wanted to show Lissa that if he ever does try to break in here, I'll be ready for him."

"Thanks, Daddy," Melissa said, pushing a tangle[2] of hair off her face.

"The gun is always here in this drawer," Mr. Dryden said, carefully putting it back and sliding the drawer shut.

"Good night," Melissa said.

"Good night." Her mother was already under the covers.

Melissa crept[3] back to her room, turned off the lamp, and climbed into bed. The tree branch was still tapping gently[4] against the windowpane. She pulled the covers up over her head and tried to ignore it[5]. She turned onto her back, then onto her side, but she couldn't fall asleep. What a terrible night! First the argument[6] with Buddy. Then the false alarm[7] about the prowler.

She thought about Buddy. She had been so glad to see him. It had been two whole weeks, after all. He looked so handsome[8] after two weeks at the beach. They had so much to talk about. So she hadn't minded[9] when he suggested they borrow his dad's car and drive up to River Ridge to talk. River Ridge, high above the Conononka River, was one of the prettiest spots in Shadyside. It was also the favorite make-out[10] spot of kids from Shadyside High. He pulled into a space overlooking the river and cut the engine and lights.

"So tell me about your vacation. Did you meet any cute girls?" Melissa teased[11]. Instead of replying, Buddy had pulled her close. They kissed.

---

1   **to yawn** – *gähnen*
2   **tangle of hair** – *Haarsträhne*
3   **to creep** – *kriechen*
4   **gentle** – *zart, sachte*
5   **to ignore sth.** – *etw. ausblenden*
6   **argument** – *Streit*
7   **false alarm** – *Fehlalarm*
8   **handsome** – *gutaussehend*
9   **She hadn't minded...** – *Sie hatte nichts dagegen gehabt …*
10 **to make out** – *rummachen*
11 **to tease** – *necken*

"Buddy, I thought we came up here to talk. I haven't seen you for weeks."

"We can talk later."

"No, Buddy—" But he slipped a hand under her blouse.

"Move your hand!" She pulled away from him. "Come on, Buddy!" She reached¹ for the door handle.

"What are you doing? I thought you'd be glad to see me."

"I said I wanted to talk."

He apologized² again and again. But as far as she was concerned³, the evening was ruined. What was the matter⁴ with him? He had never been like that before.

"Let's start over," he suggested, looking very unhappy. They tried to have a normal conversation then, but it just didn't work. Melissa still felt surprised and angry, and Buddy looked angry too. A short while later they drove home in silence. As Buddy pulled up the drive, he apologized again. He really sounded as if he were sorry. She kissed him quickly on the cheek and ran into the house, more upset with herself than with him.

Maybe she had overreacted⁵, but if only she could stop thinking and get to sleep. It must be after four in the morning. The tree limb tapped against the window, three short taps. She pictured her father removing the pistol from the bed-table drawer with that grim smile.

"The gun is always here in this drawer," he had said.

Despite the heat of the room, Melissa shuddered.

There was something so frightening about that little silver pistol, lying there in the drawer, just waiting to be used.

What has Melissa read about in the news lately and why does this make her frightened at night?

---

1 **to reach for sth.** – *nach etw. greifen*
2 **to apologize** – *sich entschuldigen*
3 **as far as she was concerned** – *was sie betraf*
4 **What was the matter with him?** – *Was war los mit ihm?*
5 **to overreact** – *überreagieren*

CHAPTER 2

Maybe I should tie my hair back¹, Melissa thought. Lying on her stomach on her bed, trying to read a book, she kept pushing it out of her face. "Why don't you get it cut before school starts?" her best friend, Delia O'Connor, had asked a few days earlier. Delia had perfect hair–straight, black, and long, and it always fell perfectly into place.

"I like it wild like this," Melissa had replied. After all, what good was hair if you couldn't toss² it, pull it, play with it? Melissa didn't want perfect hair–she wanted hair with personality! If only it would stay out of her eyes while she read.

"And why am I reading this Stephen King novel?" she asked herself. "There I was, scared silly³ by a twig⁴ on the window last night, and this afternoon I'm reading this creepy⁵ book." The room suddenly felt cold. Had she imagined it? No. She looked at the window. The afternoon sun was still high in the sky. The curtains weren't moving. There was no wind at all. She heard the front door slam⁶ downstairs.

"I'm home!" her father yelled⁷.

He's home early, she thought. What's going on?

"Lissa–are you home?"

"Yes, I'm here, Daddy." The air felt warm as soon as she left her room. Mr. Dryden watched her come down the stairs with a strange smile on his face.

"What's that smile for? Aren't you home a little early?"

He put on a phony⁸ hurt expression. "Aren't you glad to see me?"

"No. Not at all," she replied with a straight face⁹.

"Well, I think you'll be glad when you see what I have for you. Where's your mother?"

"At the mall. Where else?"

---

1 **to tie one's hair back –** *sich die Haare zusammenbinden*
2 **to toss –** *(hier:) zurückwerfen*
3 **to be scared silly –** *Todesängste ausstehen*
4 **twig –** *Zweig*
5 **creepy –** *unheimlich*
6 **to slam –** *zuknallen*
7 **to yell –** *brüllen, rufen*
8 **phony –** *vorgetäuscht*
9 **with a straight face –** *ohne eine Miene zu verziehen*

"Oh, well. I can't wait for her. I have to show you."

"Show me what? Come on!"

He laughed. "Maybe I should make you guess what your birthday surprise is."

"Birthday surprise? But my birthday isn't until Friday." She tried to think of what he could have bought[1] her. He hadn't even asked what she wanted. What did she want? She couldn't think of anything…

"Maybe I'll make you wait till Friday," he said, obviously[2] teasing. "Let's change the subject." He loosened his tie[3] and started to remove his suit jacket.

"No way!" Melissa cried. "Come on, Dad, cough it up[4]."

He reached into his pocket and dropped a set of keys into her hand. "Okay. There you go. Happy birthday!"

Melissa looked at the keys, confused[5]. "What's this?"

"Look." He pulled open the front door. Sitting in the drive[6] was a shiny blue Pontiac Firebird.

"Are you kidding[7]?" Melissa cried. "That's for me?"

He just grinned[8] and nodded his head.

"I don't believe it!" Melissa jumped up and hugged him. Then she pushed open the door and ran out to her new car.

"Well, go ahead. Sit in it," Mr. Dryden said after they had walked around it at least a dozen times.

"I can't believe this is mine," Melissa said, sitting behind the wheel. She smiled as she breathed in that wonderful new car smell. She ran her hand over the leather seat and then tried the steering wheel.

"I may want to borrow[9] it from time to time," her father said, lowering his bulky frame[10] into the passenger seat.

"Listen, Dad, this is too much."

"Yeah, you're spoiled rotten[11]. I'll keep the car after all."

---

1 **what he could have bought her** – *was er ihr gekauft haben konnte*
2 **obvious** – *offenkundig*
3 **to loosen one's tie** – *sich die Krawatte lockern*
4 **Cough it up!** – *Spuck's aus!*
5 **confused** – *verwirrt*
6 **drive** – *Auffahrt*
7 **Are you kidding?** – *(ugs.) Machst du Witze?*
8 **to grin** – *grinsen*
9 **to borrow** – *leihen*
10 **bulky frame** – *(hier:) kräftiger Körper*
11 **spoiled rotten** – *total verwöhnt*

He grabbed the keys from her hand, but she grabbed them back. "On second thoughts, what's so terrible about being spoiled rotten?" she said. She kissed him on the cheek. "I've got to show this to Delia. Can I drive it?" "It's yours. Go ahead. But don't stay too long. Your mother will be sad if she doesn't get to see it."

He's standing there watching me, she told herself, realizing she was nervous driving a beautiful new car. But she made it onto Fear Street. A few minutes later she turned up The Mill Road and drove toward the North Hills section of town[1] where Delia lived.

The car was so easy to drive. The Mill Road was pretty crowded, with people going home from work, but most of the traffic was heading the other way. She turned onto Canyon Drive to get away from the traffic and pressed down hard on the accelerator[2]. The car responded immediately with a roar and a burst of speed. She glanced[3] at the speedometer–she was doing seventy-five–so she slowed at little.

"Oh!"

She cried out as the car suddenly veered[4] to the right.

Melissa grabbed the wheel tighter, her heart pounding.

What had happened? Was the car pulling to the right? No. It happened so suddenly, with such force[5] that it felt as if someone had grabbed the wheel. She felt a sudden chill. It was warm and sunny outside, but the air in the car was extremely cold.

Melissa slowed down, keeping a tight hold on the wheel. She had just started to relax a little when the car jerked[6] again, swerving[7] wildly to the right. The tires spun onto the soft shoulder[8]. What was going on? She slowed down to twenty-five. There's something wrong with the car, she told herself.

What was that?

---

1 **section of town** – *Stadtteil*
2 **to press down on the accelerator** – *aufs Gaspedal drücken*
3 **to glance at sth.** – *einen Blick auf etw. werfen*
4 **to veer** – *(hier:) scharf ausscheren*
5 **force** – *Gewalt, Kraft*
6 **to jerk** – *ruckeln*
7 **to swerve** – *einen Schlenker machen*
8 **The tires spun onto the soft shoulder.** – *Die Reifen drehten auf dem weichen Randstreifen durch.*

It sounded like whispering[1]. A voice. Nearby. No. It couldn't be. It was the wind. Again she heard it. She shivered[2] from the cold, from surprise, from sudden fear. She gripped[3] the wheel even tighter.

What was it saying? She could hear it so clearly. A whisper right in her ear. Did it say her name?

Melisssssssssa. Just wind. Cold wind in her ear. Cold wind whispering so softly in her ear.

Melissssssssa …

Delia's house was just a few blocks away.

I can make it, she thought, ignoring the whispering wind. But again the car swerved, this time to the left, crossing the center lane[4] into the path of an oncoming[5] oil truck.

Why did Melissa not expect to get a birthday present yet?

CHAPTER 3

TR. 03

"Happy birthday, Lissa."

"Hi, Delia. You're late. Everyone's here already."

It was Friday evening. Melissa's house was filled with kids. Delia stepped into the front hallway. There was a loud crash from the den[6], followed by laughter. "Sounds like I'm just in time," Delia said, handing Melissa a present. "It's a car. I thought you could use two."

"Don't mention my new car," Melissa said, rolling her eyes. "Only two days old and in the garage already."

---

1   **whispering** – Geflüster
2   **to shiver** – zittern
3   **to grip** – packen
4   **lane** – Spur
5   **oncoming** – entgegenkommend
6   **den** – Hobbyraum

"Did they find out what's wrong with the steering[1]?"

"No. They can't find anything wrong. Daddy told them to keep looking till they find it. He's more upset than I am. And I'm the one who was almost killed by that oil truck. Hey—where's Pete?"

"Here I am." Pete Goodwin popped up behind Delia. "Happy birthday." He handed Melissa a small, flat package, obviously a CD. "Hope you like Weird Al."

"Oh, get real, Pete," Delia said, poking[2] him with her elbow. "It isn't Weird Al," she told Melissa.

"I'll put it in the other room with the other stuff," Melissa said. Pete's okay, she thought. For a long time she had wondered why Delia liked him so much. Sure, he was nice looking. But he always seemed sort of snobby and stiff[3]. But after spending a lot of time with Pete and Delia, Melissa had decided her first impressions of Pete were wrong. He was really nice and very smart, and he loosened up[4] a lot after he got to know you.

Delia, of course, looked as beautiful as ever. Her straight black hair fell softly down her back. Her silky green blouse matched her eyes. Her jeans showed off her perfect figure. Melissa tugged[5] at her frizzy blonde hair, which she had actually tried to brush before the party. I'm not going to be jealous of Delia, she thought, as she followed them into the large and noisy den—not on my birthday.

"Hey, Lissa—good party!" Marnie Foster called.

"You got any more chips?" David Metcalfe shouted. He was sitting in an armchair in the corner, holding the potato-chip bowl in his lap, stuffing his face[6]. Krissie Munroe reached out from behind the armchair, grabbed the potato-chip bowl, and dropped it over David's head. He protested loudly and blindly reached for Krissie. But she was already halfway across the room.

"Hey—where's Buddy?" Delia asked.

"He's late," shouted Melissa. "So what else is new[7]?" Buddy wasn't the most punctual[8] person in the universe. But Melissa was disappointed[9] that he

---

1 **steering** – *Steuerung*
2 **to poke** – *stupsen*
3 **stiff** – *steif, spießig*
4 **to loosen up** – *lockerer werden*
5 **to tug at sth.** – *an etw. zupfen*
6 **to stuff one's face** – *(ugs.) sich vollstopfen*
7 **So what else is new?** – *(ugs.) Na, und?*
8 **punctual** – *pünktlich*
9 **disappointed** – *enttäuscht*

wasn't on time for her birthday party. Can he still be mad at me about the other night? she wondered, glancing up at the clock. No, he had been very sorry. And he had called her the next day, and they'd had a nice long talk. Stop being so nervous, she told herself. It isn't even that late.

She thought she heard the doorbell. It was impossible to hear anything over the loud music and the even louder voices. She went out of the den, and there was Buddy, grinning at her from the doorway. He was wearing a sleeveless blue T-shirt and white tennis shorts, obviously showing off his tan. He looks great, Melissa thought, rushing up to greet him. "Hi." He kissed her quickly and pushed a small box, wrapped in silver, into her hand. "Go ahead. Open it."

"No." She squeezed his hand. "I'll open it later."

"With all the others?" He gave her his hurt[1] look. She leaned against him and whispered in his ear. "Stay after everyone's left. I'll open it then."

"Any more chips?" Metcalfe called, holding up the empty bowl.

"Turn the music up!" someone yelled. "I can still hear Metcalfe!"

A slow number[2] came on, and a few more couples started dancing. Melissa looked for Buddy, thinking he might want to dance. But he was in a corner talking to Normie Shrader. They were both demonstrating[3] forehand swings[4], so Melissa figured they were talking tennis, which both of them were fanatics about. The party was going really well. Everyone seemed to be having a great time. Melissa relaxed and enjoyed it too. The next time she looked at the clock it was past eleven-thirty.

Uh-oh, she thought. She had promised she'd try to have everyone out of the house by midnight. "Cake time!" she cried, and turned off the stereo. "Cake time! Come on. Everybody into the dining room."

Having them all sing "Happy Birthday" to her was just as embarrassing on her seventeenth birthday as it had been on all the others. But the huge chocolate cake was delicious. As she swallowed her last mouthful of cake, Melissa jumped to her feet. "You've all got to be out of here ten minutes ago!"

---

1 **hurt** – (hier:) beleidigt
2 **slow number** – Schmuselied
3 **to demonstrate** – zeigen
4 **forehand swing** – Vorhandschlag

"Party pooper[1]!" someone yelled.

"Open the presents!" David shouted.

"Okay. Sorry. I almost forgot."

"Sure. You already got a car. Why should you care[2] about our presents?" Buddy said. Melissa knew he was only joking, but for some reason, it annoyed[3] her. Her friends often gave her a hard time because her family was wealthy[4], but she didn't expect Buddy to do the same.

"Come on. I put them all in the downstairs guest bedroom," Melissa said. "We'll have to hurry. My parents will be home soon, and I promised you'd be out of here when they got back."

"We can take a hint[5]," David said. Buddy put his arm around her shoulders as she led them to the guest bedroom.

"I stacked[6] all the presents on the bed," Melissa said, "and I think we can–" She clicked on the light, looked at the bed, and gasped[7]. Everyone pushed into the room. "What's going on?"

"What happened?"

"Who did that?"

The room grew silent as everyone stared[8]. The presents were scattered[9] over the bed and floor. They had all been ripped open[10].

Melissa was kissing Buddy good night in the den when her parents walked in.

"The party's still going on?" Mrs. Dryden asked.

Buddy, embarrassed[11], pulled away from Melissa and jumped up from the couch. "I was just, uh… going."

"How was the party?" Mr. Dryden asked, walking over to the potato-chip bowl, disappointed to find it empty.

---

1 **party pooper** – *Spaßbremse*
2 **to care about sth.** – *sich für etwas interessieren*
3 **to annoy sb.** – *jdn. aufregen, stören*
4 **wealthy** – *wohlhabend*
5 **to take a hint** – *(hier:) den Wink mit dem Zaunpfahl verstehen*
6 **to stack** – *aufstapeln*
7 **to gasp** – *keuchen, nach Luft schnappen*
8 **to stare** – *starren*
9 **scattered** – *verstreut*
10 **to rip open** – *aufreißen*
11 **embarrassed** – *verlegen*

"Great!" Melissa said quickly. She had decided not to tell her parents about the presents being ripped open. Why bother them with something so silly. "I think everyone had a good time."

"Yeah, it was great," Buddy repeated, inching[1] toward the front hall. "Too bad about your rug. And the wallpaper. And those dishes."

"What?" Melissa's mother looked as if she were about to have a heart attack.

"Buddy's kidding, Mom," Melissa said. "Aren't you used to his bizarre sense of humor[2] yet?"

"Did they eat all the potato chips?" Mr. Dryden asked, turning another large plastic bowl upside down.

"When they ran out, they ate the bowls," Buddy said.

"Buddy–go home," Melissa groaned.

"Where'd you get that silver pendant[3]?" Mrs. Dryden asked, walking over and lifting it off Melissa's neck.

"Buddy gave it to me."

"Very nice." Mrs. Dryden looked at Buddy. "What good taste[4]. Did someone help you choose it?"

"Good night, everyone," Buddy said and left hastily[5].

"Strange kid," Mrs. Dryden muttered[6].

After telling them a few more details about the party and thanking them for letting her take over the house, Melissa went upstairs to bed. She felt tired, but not sleepy. The window was open. It was a cool night, the first hint that autumn was on its way. A gentle breeze[7] blew the curtains out, then they fell back. The air smelled sweet and fresh.

The streetlight at the end of the yard[8] cast a yellow light in the room. Melissa stared at the moving shadows on the wall. Who could have done it? she wondered. Who ripped open her presents and left them all over the room?

---

1   **to inch towards sth.** – *sich etw. in kleinen Schritten nähern*
2   **bizarre sense of humor** – *merkwürdiger Humor*
3   **pendant** – *Anhänger*
4   **good taste** – *guter Geschmack*
5   **hasty** – *hastig*
6   **to mutter** – *murmeln*
7   **breeze** – *Brise*
8   **yard** – *(hier:) Garten vor dem Haus*

Her friends all seemed shocked by the sight[1] in the guest bedroom. She hadn't seen any of them leave the den or living room. Besides, they were her friends, all people who liked her. No one there would do anything that mean[2] to her. The only other person in the house was Marta, the housekeeper. But she was busy in the kitchen, working to keep the food for the party coming, and washing the plates and glasses. It couldn't have been Marta.

Then who? And more importantly, why? Why would someone sneak into the bedroom and tear open every package? To ruin the party? Just to make Melissa feel bad?

It made no sense at all.

Melissa ran her hand over the silver pendant Buddy had given her. It felt cool and smooth in her hand. I'm going to wear it all the time, she thought. I'm never going to take it off. Even her mother had been impressed by it. Suddenly the room felt cold again. She sat up and started to climb out of bed. Such a chilling cold to come on so suddenly.

She lowered her feet to the carpet and looked up. A young man stepped out of the shadows at the foot of her bed. She couldn't see his face. The light from the window formed an outline[3] around his dark form. She could see that he had long, dark hair, narrow shoulders[4]. He had no face. Only the blackness of night where his face should have been.

"Who are you? What are you doing here?" she cried.

He didn't reply. He moved around the bed, walking slowly toward her. The Fear Street Prowler, she thought. She drew in her breath[5] and screamed at the top of her lungs.

Why is everyone shocked when they walk into the guest room?

---

1 **sight** –*Anblick*
2 **mean** – *gemein*
3 **outline** – *Umriss*
4 **narrow shoulders** – *schmale Schultern*
5 **She drew in her breath...** – *Sie atmete tief ein ...*

CHAPTER 4

As the dark figure moved closer, his features[1] remained hidden in shadow. He looked to Melissa as if he had no face at all. The shadow was moving forward, arms raised, to engulf[2] her.

"Melissa–what on earth!" Her father burst into the room.

"He's in here, Daddy! He's in here!" Melissa cried out. Finally the light came on. Her father stood against the wall, his face filled with confusion, frantically[3] looking around the room.

"Where, Lissa?"

"Who?" Seeing no one, her father walked over to her bed and slumped down[4] on the edge.

"Daddy, he–"

"I don't see anyone."

"What happened? Why did she scream again?" Mrs. Dryden came into the room. She was still dressed, and hadn't even taken off her shoes.

Melissa climbed out of bed. "I'm not crazy! Someone was in this room." Mr. Dryden stood up and walked quickly to the window. "Did he jump out the window?"

"Wes, don't lean out like that!" Mrs. Dryden called, clutching at her throat, frightened. He pulled his head back in and turned to Melissa, who was standing right beside him. He shook his head. "I don't see anyone."

"Who was in here? A man? What did he look like? Call the police, Wes."

"How can I call the police? There's no one here." He looked at Melissa.

"He… he disappeared," Melissa said uncertainly[5]. "I saw him. He was as close to me as you are. I saw him clearly. I didn't make it up. I wasn't dreaming."

"And then he disappeared into thin air[6]?"

"I–I don't know."

---

1 **features** – *Gesichtszüge*
2 **to engulf** – *umfassen*
3 **frantically** – *hektisch, panisch*
4 **to slump down** – *in sich zusammensacken*
5 **uncertain** – *unsicher*
6 **to disappear into thin air** – *sich in Luft auflösen*

"Well, what did he look like? Can you describe him?" her mother demanded.

"Well, he…" Melissa's mouth dropped open. She pulled at a curly strand of hair[1] as she thought. "It was too dark," she said finally. "I couldn't see his face. I could just see–"

"What? What could you see?" her mother asked.

"I could see that he had long hair."

"And?"

"That's all," Melissa said quietly. She knew it sounded stupid. But it was the truth. Why were they doubting[2] her? Couldn't they see how frightened she was? Her father walked over to comfort her, as if reading her mind[3]. "You've got to control your imagination," he said softly, smoothing her hair with one hand. "Last time–"

"Last time was a tree branch," Melissa said, becoming impatient[4], "tonight was real."

"If he was real, where is he? Why can't you describe him?" asked her mother.

"I told you," she said angrily. "It was too dark. I could only see his outline. He raised his arms. He moved toward me. And then Daddy came in."

"And he vanished into thin air." Mrs. Dryden shook her head. "It's just the excitement over your birthday, the new car. It all caught up with you, that's all."

"Please, Mother. Don't talk to me like I'm a baby."

"Come on, Lissa." Mr. Dryden held out his arms. "There's no need to be angry at us."

"You don't believe me, do you?" Melissa snapped[5].

"Well, no," her father said, glancing at her mother. "I think the stories about the Fear Street Prowler have upset you enough to think that you're seeing him in your room. I believe that you really saw what you said you saw. But I think your mind was playing tricks on you[6]. I think–"

"That I'm crazy?"

"No. Of course not," her mother broke in. "Let me make you some warm milk. It will make you feel sleepy."

---

1 **strand of hair** – *Haarsträhne*
2 **to doubt sb.** – *(hier:) an jds. Verstand zweifeln*
3 **as if reading her mind** – *als ob er in ihre Gedanken lesen könnte*
4 **impatient** – *ungeduldig*
5 **to snap** – *(hier:) fauchen*
6 **to play tricks on sb.** – *jdm. Streiche spielen*

"Good night, you two," said Melissa wearily¹. She gave them a tired wave and climbed back into bed. "I'm feeling calm now. I'm sorry I disturbed² you." Her mother started out³ the door, looking very troubled⁴. Her father followed, but stopped at the doorway. "Shall I close the window? Will that make you feel better?"

Melissa shook her head. "The breeze feels nice. It's the first cool night we've had."

"Shall I turn off the lamp?"

"Yeah. Thanks. 'Night, Daddy. 'Night, Mom."

They muttered good night and walked out into the hall. A few seconds later Melissa could hear her parents talking about her in their room across the hall. She stared up at the ceiling. It seemed to be glowing, pale yellow from the light coming in through the window.

I'm wide-awake⁵ now, she thought. I'll never get to sleep tonight. She sat up, then climbed out of bed. It was so bright⁶ in her room. She didn't remember the streetlight being that bright before. She walked to the window and pulled the curtains to the side. The air was refreshing. Resting her hands lightly on the window ledge⁷, she leaned out. It was such a clear night. Through the trees that lined both sides of the narrow street, she could almost see the jagged⁸ outlines of Simon Fear's burned-out old mansion⁹ at the far end of the street.

Melissa's friends were always telling her terrible stories about Fear Street. But she loved the neighborhood¹⁰. Her parents loved anything old and interesting, and they had passed their enthusiasm on to Melissa. Fear Street is by far the most interesting street in Shadyside, she thought.

Looking up, she saw the full moon. Its pale light reflected off the silver pendant around her neck. How beautiful, she thought. She stretched farther

---

1 **weary** – erschöpft, müde
2 **to disturb** – stören
3 **to start out** – herausgehen
4 **troubled** – bekümmert
5 **wide-awake** – hellwach
6 **bright** – hell
7 **window ledge** – Fensterbank (an der Außenseite des Gebäudes)
8 **jagged** – kantig
9 **mansion** – Anwesen
10 **neighborhood** – Viertel

out the window, leaning on both hands. What was that running across the grass in the yard across the street? Was it a rabbit? I'd better get back to bed, she thought. I'll be totally wrecked[1] tomorrow.

But as she started to straighten up, she felt two powerful hands on her back. Before she could cry out, the two hands shoved[2] her hard, shoved her with startling[3], almost inhuman[4] power.

Does Melissa's father think she is lying about what she saw in her room?

CHAPTER 5

TR. 05

Gripping the window frame[5] tightly, she regained her balance and pushed back, resisting the steady[6] force on her back.

Her attacker shoved even harder.

The hands felt so cold on her back. The air felt so cold. Gathering all her strength[7], she turned to face her attacker. But there was no one there. She stared into the darkness of her room, panting[8] loudly, each breath a cry of pain, of terror, of relief[9].

Where are you? she thought. Where did you go? How did you disappear so quickly? He must still be in the room. But where? Her legs trembled[10]. She felt sick and was covered in a cold sweat.

"Hey–I know you're here!" she croaked[11].

---

1 **wrecked –** *(ugs.) platt, fix und fertig*
2 **to shove –** *schubsen*
3 **startling –** *überraschend*
4 **inhuman –** *übermenschlich*
5 **frame –** *Rahmen*
6 **steady –** *beständig*
7 **to gather one's strength –** *seine Kräfte zusammennehmen*
8 **to pant –** *keuchen, schnauben*
9 **relief –** *Erleichterung*
10 **to tremble –** *zittern, beben*
11 **to croak –** *krächzen*

Somehow she made it to the bed and turned on the lamp. She looked around the room. No one was there.

"I know you're here."

On trembling legs she walked to the closet and opened both doors. No one.

"I know you're here."

She dropped to the floor and looked under the bed. No one.

Should she call for her dad? No. He would only come running in to find the room empty once again. She'd get those looks again from both her parents that said they were starting to think there was something seriously wrong with her. Well, was there? Was she going crazy?

I almost went flying out that window, she thought. Someone tried to push me out that window. I didn't imagine it. I didn't dream it. I'm not cracking up[1]. She pulled herself back into bed, drew the covers up to her chin. There's no one here, she thought. I'm safe now. Perfectly safe.

A few minutes later she fell asleep with the light on.

When a cold shadow drifted up to her bed and hovered[2] over her, she didn't awaken.

* * *

Buddy was cleaning the garage when Melissa arrived.

"Didn't you just clean the garage a few weeks ago?" she asked, moving aside as he threw a wooden basket full of garden trowels[3] and pruning shears[4] onto the drive.

"Yeah. But my dad said I didn't do a good enough job."

"You're tossing everything out, then bringing everything back in?"

"Yeah. But neatly."

He was wearing a stained[5], plain-white T-shirt with faded jean cutoffs[6], and white sneakers with no socks. He looks great, Melissa thought. "You should keep that tan all-year-round," she said.

---

1 **to crack up** – (ugs.) durchdrehen
2 **to hover** – schweben
3 **trowel** – Schaufel
4 **pruning shear** – Gartenschere
5 **stained** – gefleckt
6 **jean cutoffs** – abgeschnittene Jeans

He laughed. "Yeah. Maybe I'll go to one of those tanning places every week and barbecue¹ myself." He picked up a large bag of soil² and carried it out to the driveway.

"You didn't notice that I'm wearing your pendant," she said, running her hand over it.

"Sure, I noticed." He wiped the sweat off his forehead with his arm. "Go on with what you were telling me on the phone earlier."

"Nothing more to tell. There was someone in my room. And my parents both think I'm crazy." She waited for him to say something, but he only picked up a ladder and carried it past her.

"You think I'm crazy too?"

"Maybe it was the wind. Or shadows or something."

"Shadows don't push you out windows," she snapped angrily. "I'm not crazy, Buddy."

"I'm just trying to figure out what it could be."

"Me too. And what about the birthday presents? I just keep seeing them, all ripped up like that. Who could've done such a stupid, horrible thing?"

He shrugged³. "I don't know."

"I'm kind of frightened. It's all too weird."

"You have to chill out⁴."

"What's that mean?" she snapped. Then she realized how hard Buddy was trying to be understanding. "Sorry," she said, "I–I just wish they'd catch that Fear Street Prowler. I keep thinking he's going to come climbing in and–"

"What makes you think he'll come to your house?"

"I don't know. I think maybe he's already been there."

Buddy shook his head. "Oh, right. He climbed in, opened all your presents, and left. That makes a lot of sense⁵."

She playfully⁶ pushed him away with both hands. "Thanks for all the support. I've got to go."

"Where to?"

---

1   **to barbecue** – *grillen*
2   **soil** – *Erde*
3   **to shrug** – *mit den Achseln zucken*
4   **Chill out!** – *(ugs.) Beruhige dich!*
5   **That makes a lot of sense** – *(ironisch) Ja, klar doch.*
6   **playful** – *scherzhaft*

"I promised Delia I'd meet her at the mall. I have a little money. I thought maybe I'd buy some clothes for school. See you later. What time are you picking me up¹?"

"Hey, why don't you pick me up? You're the one with the awesome car," he replied.

She laughed. "I knew you were going to say that. Okay. Pick you up at eight–if my car is fixed and out of the garage." She climbed into her mother's Volvo and, feeling a little cheered up², waved goodbye to Buddy.

* * *

After dropping Delia off in North Hills, she drove the Volvo down Park Drive toward Fear Street. She had enjoyed shopping with Delia and was happy, but then suddenly, she heard the whispering sound. Again. The sound of air, whispering her name.

"Melisssssssssa."

"Oh!" she cried out.

"Melisssssssssa."

No. Not again. What on earth could be making that sound?

The car suddenly felt cold, the same chilling, damp³ cold she had felt in her new car.

"Melisssssssssssa."

And suddenly there he was, in the passenger seat beside her. A young man, probably about her age. Tough looking. With black, greasy⁴ hair down to his collar. And dark, dangerous eyes. Dressed all in blue denim. Melissa cried out, and crashed into the car ahead of her.

> **Does Buddy think that Melissa is in danger?**

---

1   **to pick sb. up** – *jdn. abholen*
2   **cheered up** – *aufgemuntert*
3   **damp** – *feucht*
4   **greasy** – *fettig, schmierig*

CHAPTER 6

The driver of the car Melissa hit—a large, middle-aged man in a business suit—came storming¹ out of his car, red-faced and angry. Melissa didn't move until he tapped on her window, three hard taps with the back of his hand. She rolled down the window, but didn't get out. "Weren't you watching?" the man asked, his face growing even redder. "I was stopped for the light." "Sorry," she said, feeling a little better. "Are you okay?"

"Why didn't you stop?" the man demanded angrily, ignoring her question. "Are you stoned² or something?" He stared at her, examining her eyes.

"No. I just didn't see—I mean, this boy popped up³ beside me and I was so surprised—"

"Boy?" The man leaned down to the window and peered past Melissa to the passenger side. Melissa turned to the passenger seat, then looked at the backseat. There was no one there.

"Hey—where are you?" she said. "Where'd you go?" She turned back to the man. "I'm sorry. He was here. Really."

He threw up his hands impatiently. "I can't listen to this nonsense. I'm late for a meeting." He left her window to go examine his rear bumper⁴. Melissa reluctantly pushed open the car door and stepped outside. She felt a little shaky⁵, but took a few steps and began to feel better.

"Your car isn't even dented⁶," the man said, rubbing his chin, his face still nearly tomato red.

"And what about your car?" Melissa asked, thinking about the boy with the long hair. The boy looked so tough, so angry. She could see that even in the brief glimpse⁷ she got of him. Have I seen him some place before?

---

1 **to storm out –** *herausstürmen*
2 **stoned –** *bekifft*
3 **to pop up –** *erscheinen*
4 **bumper –** *Stoßstange*
5 **shaky –** *zitterig, wackelig auf den Beinen*
6 **dented –** *verbeult*
7 **brief glimpse –** *flüchtiger Blick*

"Just a scratch[1]," the man said, getting down on his knees to look under the car. "I guess we're both okay."

"My parents have insurance[2]."

"No need. Let's just forget about this, okay?" He smiled for the first time. His face started to return to a normal color. He stretched[3] and rolled his head around. "Neck seems to be okay. Guess we were lucky."

"I guess," Melissa said doubtfully[4]. "I'm really sorry. You're being so nice about this."

"I'm a nice guy," he said, getting back into his car. "Do me a favor, though. Drive behind someone else from now on."

"Oh. Sure." Melissa wasn't certain if he was joking or not. She watched him pull away, thinking about the long-haired boy. She could see him so clearly, his dark eyes, his nervous frown. She couldn't have imagined him.

"I'm really worried about you, Lissa. You're obviously extremely—"

"No, I'm not overtired, Mother." Melissa tore a piece off her roll but didn't eat it. She hadn't intended[5] to tell her parents about the accident, but during a long silence, it just came out. Now she was sorry she had told them.

"This young man you say you saw," her father asked thoughtfully, "did he look like the young man that you claimed you saw[6] in your room last night?"

"Why'd you have to say claimed?" Melissa shrieked[7], sounding more angry that she meant. "You really think I'm crazy, don't you? Claimed! Claimed! That's the kind of thing you say to someone in one of your court cases[8], Daddy. I'm not your client. I'm your daughter!"

She knew she had gone too far. She couldn't help it.

"Calm down, dear. Try to eat." Mrs. Dryden hated scenes of any kind, especially at the dinner table.

---

1   **scratch –** *Kratzer*
2   **to have insurance –** *versichert sein*
3   **to stretch –** *sich strecken*
4   **doubtful –** *skeptisch*
5   **She hadn't intended to… –** *Sie hatte nicht vorgehabt, …*
6   **that you claimed you saw –** *den du gesehen haben willst*
7   **to shriek –** *kreischen*
8   **court case –** *Gerichtsverfahren*

"I'm sorry. I didn't mean …" Her father pulled off his glasses and rubbed his nose. His eyes looked so much smaller with his glasses off. He suddenly looked very tired.

"Your dad had a really good idea this afternoon," Mrs. Dryden said to Melissa, finishing the last piece of salmon[1] on her plate.

Here she goes, changing the subject again, Melissa thought. For once, however, Melissa was relieved[2].

"Why don't you tell her?" Mrs. Dryden asked her husband.

Mr. Dryden swallowed a mouthful of potatoes. "Excellent dinner tonight. Remind me to tell Marta."

"I hear you. Thanks for the compliment[3]!" Marta called through the closed kitchen door. Marta probably thinks I'm crazy too, Melissa thought gloomily.

"Go ahead. Tell Melissa your idea," her mother urged.

"Well, your mom and I have to go to this lawyers' convention[4]," Mr. Dryden started. "It's next weekend in Las Vegas. We're leaving Thursday night to make it a long weekend. And I thought maybe you'd like to come too."

"It'll be really good for you," her mother said quickly, before Melissa had a chance to react. "You need a change of scenery. School doesn't start until–"

"I really don't want to," Melissa interrupted[5].

"Why not, Lissa?" Mr. Dryden asked, very disappointed.

"I just don't want to go to Las Vegas with a bunch of lawyers. What would I do while you and Mom are at your meetings and parties? I'm not old enough for the casinos."

"But, Melissa," Mrs. Dryden argued, "there's tennis, and swimming, and all the shows. I really think you'd have a great time. You need to get out of this house."

"Sorry," Melissa said, getting up from the table.

"Where are you going?" Mrs. Dryden asked angrily.

"I have a date with Buddy. I'm picking him up. He'll be so surprised to see my new car is back." She gave her father a quick kiss on the forehead. "Thanks for picking it up for me, Daddy." He smiled up at her forgivingly[6].

---

1 **salmon** – *Lachs*
2 **relieved** – *erleichtert*
3 **compliment** – *Kompliment*
4 **convention** – *Messe, Tagung*
5 **to interrupt** – *unterbrechen*
6 **forgiving** – *verzeihend*

"I really think you should reconsider¹," Mrs. Dryden called. Melissa didn't reply, but hurried up to her room.

She showered quickly, then put on a red sweater and a new pair of jeans. She was putting Buddy's silver pendant around her neck when the boy appeared beside her.

His dark eyes stared into hers. She could see him clearly now. He had long, dark brown hair that looked as if it hadn't been washed in weeks. He had thick, dark eyebrows, high cheekbones², and a mouth that seemed to fall naturally into an unpleasant sneer³. He was wearing a faded blue denim jacket and blue denim jeans.

Melissa wasn't frightened this time, just angry.

"Who are you?" she demanded, taking a step toward him. He seemed surprised, but didn't reply.

"You made me dent⁴ my mom's car," she said.

"So? You can just buy another one—right?" he said bitterly. His voice was softer than she'd imagined⁵.

"Who are you?" she repeated, refusing to back down⁶. He seemed to find her anger funny. He looked past her⁷ to the window. Then he walked over to her dressing table and stared down at her makeup and the other items.

"You don't remember me?"

"No. Why should I remember you?" she asked, feeling afraid again.

"You should remember me," he said, rushing⁸ forward and pushing his face up close to hers. "You should remember me—you killed me!"

What do Melissa's parents suggest to get her out of the house?

---

1 **to reconsider sth.** – *noch einmal über etw. nachdenken*
2 **high cheekbones** – *hohe Wangenknochen*
3 **sneer** – *spöttisches Lächeln*
4 **to dent** – *verbeulen*
5 **to imagine** – *(hier:) sich vorstellen*
6 **to back down** – *zurückweichen*
7 **to look past sb.** – *an jdm. vorbeischauen*
8 **to rush forward** – *vorstürmen*

CHAPTER 7

She backed away from him, and tripped on her sneakers and fell over. As he sneered down at her, she noticed that he had tattoos on the back of his right hand, but she couldn't see what they were. She jumped back to her feet and they stared at each other across her bed. "I've never seen you before," she said.

"Convenient," he muttered bitterly.

"I don't know what you're talking about. Stop being so mysterious[1]." He seemed to find that very funny.

"I'm not. I told you straight out[2]—you killed me. Take a good look. Remember me now?"

"You're crazy. If you're dead, how can you be standing here now? What are you—a ghost[3]?"

What should she do? Run from the room? Call for her father? No. She wanted some answers.

"Don't play innocent[4]." He turned his back on her. "You mean that you killed me and didn't even notice? You mean you're so rich that—"

"I didn't kill you!" Melissa screamed. "If I killed you, how did I do it?"

His hands coiled into fists[5]. "I don't remember," he said in a flat, emotionless[6] voice. "Most of my memories are gone. But I know one thing for sure. You killed me."

"That's ridiculous," Melissa cried. "Tell me the truth!"

"I'm dead," he said, turning around. His angry expression had softened. "I'm dead because you killed me."

His words chilled[7] her. He wasn't joking. But what he was saying was impossible.

---

1 **mysterious** – *rätselhaft*
2 **straight out** – *geradewegs hinaus*
3 **ghost** – *Geist*
4 **to play innocent** – *(ugs.) den/die Unschuldige spielen*
5 **His hands coiled into fists.** – *Er ballte die Hände zu Fäusten*
6 **emotionless** – *emotionslos*
7 **to chill sb.** – *jdm. einen Schauer über den Rücken jagen*

"You're as alive as I am!" she cried. She walked over to him and grabbed his arm. Her hand seemed to go right through him. All she felt was a wisp of cold air[1].

"Oh, no!" she cried, covering her mouth with her hand. She stepped back. Her heart was pounding now. She felt cold all over. She tried to scream. No sound came out.

He smiled, a grim smile. Her horrified reaction seemed to please him. "You believe me now."

"You're–you're a ghost." She wanted to run, but her legs were trembling. She felt weak all over. She slumped down onto the bed and stared up at him.

"Now you believe in ghosts," he said, his smile fading[2]. "Isn't it amazing how a few seconds can change your life. Or end it?"

"But I know I didn't kill you," Melissa insisted[3]. "It isn't something I'd forget, you know."

"You did." He pulled out the chair in front of her dressing table and sat down on it

"I can't remember how, but you killed me."

"Why? Why did I kill you?" Melissa asked.

He'd be good-looking if he washed his hair and stopped sneering like that, she thought.

"I don't remember," he said with some sadness.

"What's your name?"

"Paul."

"Paul what?"

"I don't remember."

"Huh? You don't remember your own last name?"

"I told you, I don't have much memory. Death screws you up[4] in a lot of ways, you know!" He slammed both hands against the chair. They didn't make a sound. "I can't control it. I can hardly remember anything."

---

1 **wisp of cold air** – *kalter Luftzug*
2 **to fade** – *(hier:) verblassen*
3 **to insist** – *beharren*
4 **to screw sb. up** – *(ugs.) jdn. aus der Bahn werfen*

"If you have no memory, what makes you think I killed you? You're haunting[1] the wrong house, Paul."

"No. It's one of the few things I do know. You killed me, Melissa. I do know one other thing too."

"What?"

"I know why I've come back." He stood up and started[2] toward her. "I've come back to pay you back. I've come back to kill you!"

"No!"

She jumped off the bed and started backing toward the bedroom door. He's crazy, she thought. Totally crazy. He stared into her eyes. "Scared, huh?"

"I-I'll scream."

"You screamed before. It didn't do you much good. And you can't run from a ghost, Melissa. Haven't you seen any horror movies?"

"You're making a big mistake. I didn't kill you. Really."

She was only a few steps from the door. She could be out of the room and down the steps in seconds. But then what?

"You've got to believe me," she said. "I never knew you!"

He didn't say anything, just shook his head, staring coldly at her. She realized she was shivering all over. It was freezing cold in the room. The sudden[3] cold last night. The sudden cold in the car. He brought it, she realized. He moved quickly. Before she could get through the door, he was right in front of her. His face was inches[4] from hers. He was so cold, so terribly, sickeningly[5] cold.

"I didn't do it, Paul!" Her voice came out choked[6].

"You're a liar," he said quietly, and his handsome face suddenly turned quite ugly. "A rich liar. And rich liars have to die!"

What convinces Melissa that Paul really is a ghost?

---

1 **to haunt –** *heimsuchen*
2 **to start toward sb. –** *auf jdn. losgehen*
3 **sudden –** *plötzlich*
4 **inch –** *Zoll (US-amerikanische/britische Maßeinheit)*
5 **sickening –** *entsetzlich, ekelhaft*
6 **choked –** *erstickt*

"*No*, wait–" Melissa pleaded[1], raising her hands.

"Wait for what?"

Melissa thought frantically. How could she save her life?

"Take your time[2]," he said. "I'm not going anywhere."

She slowly lowered her hands. "Maybe I could help you somehow."

A bitter smile crossed his face. It was so cold, so damp.

"I can help you. I can … uh … I can find the *real* person who killed you."

Where were her parents? Didn't they hear her talking? If only one of them would come into her room, Paul would surely disappear the way he had in the past.

"I already told you, Melissa," he said, making fun of her name as he said it. "I know who killed me. You did."

"But you're wrong. Besides …" She was thinking fast now. "Don't you want to find out how you died? Or why?"

He looked away. He was thinking about what she said.

"I could help you," she added quickly, encouraged by his silence. "I'll do everything I can to find the truth. Really."

He looked at her skeptically[3].

"Really," she repeated. "Really, I can help you. If you'll just give me a chance."

If only he'd back away. She was so cold, so freezing, shivering, shaking cold!

"Okay," he said. "There's no rush[4]. I can kill you anytime I want."

Then he was gone. And only the cold remained.

A few minutes later, she drove her new car down the drive and started towards Buddy's house. It was a warm night, the temperature still in the seventies, but she closed the car windows and turned the heater up.

She had considered telling her parents what had happened. But she quickly decided not to. Even if they didn't think she had gone bananas[5], they might

---

1 **to plead –** *flehen*
2 **Take your time. –** *Lass dir Zeit.*
3 **skeptical –** *skeptisch, misstrauisch*
4 **There's no rush. –** *Wir haben's nicht eilig.*
5 **to go bananas –** *verrückt werden*

make her lie down or even call a doctor. Buddy was a lot more likely[1] to listen to her than her mom and dad – and believe her. She hoped. Thinking about Paul, she drove through a red light. Luckily, there were no other cars nearby. I've got to concentrate on driving, she warned herself. But how? She was being haunted by a ghost, a ghost who had come back for revenge[2]. Where have I seen him before? Do I know him? Have I ever seen him? She searched her memory. No. No. No. I've never seen him in my life. I don't know anyone named Paul. I've never seen him around school. I don't remember any boy at Shadyside High being killed. No. He's wrong. She suddenly felt a shiver creep down her spine[3] despite the scorching heat inside the car.

"Paul–are you here?" she asked aloud.

Silence. No whispering of her name. Complete silence. She sighed[4] loudly, very relieved. Then she thought: What if he is here but isn't answering?

A horn honked angrily. She looked back to see why, and realized she had passed a stop sign. I shouldn't be driving, she thought.

She was almost at Buddy's house. He could drive them to the movies. But how could she go to the movies? She couldn't concentrate on a movie. She had to do something.

Maybe Buddy would know what.

A few minutes later he met her at his front door. "Hi. Where've you been?" He looked at his watch.

"It's a long story," she said. "Aren't you going to invite me in[5]?"

"We'll be late for the movie." He stepped onto the front stoop[6] beside her.

"I don't want to go to the movie. I want to talk."

He looked past her to the drive. "You got your car back. Can I drive it?"

"Yeah. Sure. But you weren't listening to me. I really want to talk."

"Well, my sister has some friends over, and my parents have company[7] too." He took her arm. "Why don't we take a drive and talk?"

---

1   **Buddy was a lot more likely to listen to her...**– *Buddy würde ihr viel eher zuhören ...*
2   **revenge** – *Rache, Vergeltung*
3   **spine** – *(hier:) Rücken*
4   **to sigh** – *seufzen*
5   **to invite sb. in** – *jdn. hereinbitten*
6   **stoop** – *Veranda*
7   **to have company** – *Besuch haben*

"Okay," she said. She finally felt warm again, but the terror of the scene in her bedroom lingered[1] in her mind. She took Buddy's arm. "Okay. Let's go."

"Why don't we drive up to River Ridge?" he asked, a sly[2] smile crossing his face.

"No. I mean it, Buddy. I really need to talk to you."

The smile disappeared immediately. "Is everything okay?"

"No," she told him.

"You mean it's about us? You want to talk about us?"

She shook her head. He's an okay guy, she thought. I really do care[3] about him. But he sure can be self-centered sometimes. He held open the passenger door and she got in. It was still hot inside the car. She turned off the heater as he walked around to the driver's side. They wouldn't be needing it now. A few minutes later they were driving slowly along Canyon Road, passing houses with neat, small lawns[4]. "I don't know where to start," Melissa said, leaning her head on his shoulder.

"This car really handles[5] great," he said. "What's the problem, Lissa?"

"Do you remember anyone named Paul at school? Someone named Paul who was killed?"

"Killed?" He turned his head to give her a confused look.

"Yeah. Killed. I don't know his last name"

Buddy thought. "No, no one from school has been killed."

"I didn't think so." She replied.

"Well, who is this guy, anyway?"

"I don't know. But remember I told you there was someone in my room and then we couldn't find anyone?"

"Yeah. Of course I remember."

"Well ..." She stopped. Would he laugh at her? Would he think she was nuts[6]? Or would he believe her? It was too late now. She had to tell him – and convince[7] him.

---

1 **to linger –** *anhalten*
2 **sly –** *gerissen*
3 **to care about sb. –** *sich aus jdm. etw. machen*
4 **lawn –** *Rasen*
5 **to handle great –** *(bei Autos) sich hervorragend fahren*
6 **to be nuts –** *(ugs.) einen Knall haben*
7 **to convince sb. –** *jdn. überzeugen*

She told him the whole story, speaking so quickly that she was out of breath by the time she told Buddy how she persuaded[1] the ghost to let her help him, to let her live for a while.

They were outside of Shadyside now, in the country. Buddy pulled the car off the road onto the shoulder[2], and turned to her. He put a warm arm around her shoulder. "Lissa–you're shaking!"

"I-I'm so scared, Buddy."

He didn't say anything. Just stared at her.

"Well, say something. What do you think?" she demanded.

The full moon was low over the flat farm fields. Thin wisps of gray blue clouds floated[3] in front of it, and it suddenly grew darker.

"At first I thought you were joking," Buddy said.

"I'm not," she said quickly.

"No. I see." He stared out through the windshield[4]. He seemed to be thinking hard. Finally he said, "You really don't believe in ghosts, do you?"

Melissa took a deep breath. She didn't want to cry in front of him. "I knew you wouldn't believe me," she whispered, her face turned away from him. He took her hand, which was cold and wet. "Melissa, I'm really worried about you. I think we have to get you some help right away."

"You won't believe me?"

"How can I? It's not possible. It's just not possible."

"Okay," Melissa said, crossing her arms[5] and facing forward. "Drive back to my house. Come on. Let's go. I'm going to prove[6] to you that I'm telling the truth."

Why does Buddy not invite Melissa into the house?

---

1 **to persuade sb.** – *jdn. überreden, überzeugen*
2 **shoulder** – *(hier:) Randstreifen*
3 **to float** – *schweben*
4 **windshield** – *Windschutzscheibe*
5 **to cross one's arms** – *die Arme verschränken*
6 **to prove sth. to sb.** – *jdm. etw. beweisen*

CHAPTER 9

TR. 09

"The car's gone. I guess my parents went out." Melissa opened the front door and Buddy followed her into the house. Melissa walked to the living room and flicked the light switch. "I hate a dark house," she said.

"Lissa, sit down," he said softly, pointing[1] to the couch.

"No," she said, shaking her head. "Come on up to my room. I want you to meet Paul."

"But this is a waste of time," he said. "There's no such thing as[2] ghosts, even on Fear Street."

"Fear Street has nothing to do with it," Melissa said.

"But the Fear Street Prowler does," Buddy said. "You've been so upset about those news stories—"

Suddenly they heard floorboards[3] squeaking[4] in the front hall. Footsteps. Buddy looked at her, his eyes wide with surprise—and fear.

Was it the prowler? Was it Melissa's ghost? Melissa stared back at Buddy. Neither of them moved. The footsteps grew louder.

They both turned to the living-room entranceway as Marta walked into the room with a pile of towels

"Hi, Marta. It's only us," Melissa said, looking at Buddy, who seemed very relieved.

"Your parents went to the Daltons'," Marta said. "I was just going to take these towels upstairs, then go to bed."

Marta disappeared. They listened to her climb the stairs.

"You can close your mouth now," Melissa told Buddy.

"I … she … I just wasn't expecting …" He laughed.

"You were expecting to see the ghost," Melissa said. "See? You do believe me." His expression turned serious. "Lissa, please. Please stop talking about this ghost. Let's try to figure out[5] what you really saw. You know, you might have dreamed the whole thing. It's possible, isn't it?"

---

1 **to point to sth. –** *auf etw. zeigen*
2 **There's no such thing as ghosts. –** *Es gibt keine Geister.*
3 **floorboard –** *Diele*
4 **to squeak –** *quietschen*
5 **to figure sth. out –** *etw. herauskriegen*

"Aaggh!" she cried out. "How could I have dreamed it? I was wide-awake!"

"But maybe you were asleep and didn't realize—"

"Come on upstairs," she said, walking quickly from the room. "When you see the ghost with your own eyes, maybe you won't think I'm crazy."

They passed Marta, who was heading down the stairs to her room in the back. She said good night as they went up. Melissa hesitated¹ at the door to her room. She looked back at Buddy, then stepped in and switched on the lamp.

"Well, where is he?" Buddy asked, speaking loudly even though he was standing right next to Melissa.

"He's here. I'm sure of it," Melissa said, walking toward the window. Buddy sat down on the bed and lay back, his hands behind his head.

"Hey—we're all alone up here," he said.

"No, we're not," Melissa said quietly. "Paul?" she called. "Paul, are you here?" She looked around the room. They both listened in silence. Outside they could hear a car drive past, its radio playing loudly.

"Paul, I brought someone to meet you," Melissa said. "I brought someone else who can help you."

Silence.

She turned back to the bed to see if Buddy was laughing at her. If he was laughing, she promised² herself, she would never speak to him again. But Buddy did not look amused. He was staring at her with concern³.

"Paul?" Melissa refused⁴ to give up. "Come on, Paul" she repeated. "I can tell he's here. It's so cold in the room," Melissa said with a shiver.

"Come over here. I'll warm you up." Buddy grinned and patted the bed again.

"Paul? Are you here, Paul?" Melissa couldn't hide⁵ the desperation⁶ from her voice. He had to show himself⁷ now. Or else Buddy would believe she really was crazy. She sat down on the edge of the bed. Buddy put his arm around her gently.

"Hey—you're freezing cold."

"Aren't you cold?" she asked. "Don't you feel it too?"

---

1   **to hesitate** – *zögern*
2   **to promise** – *versprechen*
3   **concern** – *Besorgnis*
4   **to refuse to do sth.** – *sich weigern, etw. zu tun*
5   **to hide** – *verstecken*
6   **desperation** – *Verzweiflung*
7   **to show oneself** – *sich zeigen*

"Not really," he said, pulling her head down onto his shoulder. "It's a warm August night."

It felt good to snuggle[1] against him. Melissa closed her eyes. Buddy put both arms around her. He pressed his face against hers. "I keep thinking maybe this is a gag," he said softly. "Some kind of practical joke[2] you're playing on me. Except that's really not like you."

"It's no joke," Melissa said, starting to feel angry again.

"Paul–please! Where are you?" she called.

Buddy pulled her face close to his and started to kiss her.

"No, Buddy." She pulled back. "I'm really not in the mood."

"Sshhh. Come on," he said. He kissed her again, pressing his mouth against hers. He wrapped his arms around her tightly. He felt so warm, so safe. For a brief second she lost herself in the kiss.

Then she opened her eyes and looked up. There was Paul, standing over them, watching them kiss, his dark eyes flaring[3], his mouth twisted[4] angrily. As Melissa tried to pull away from Buddy's embrace, Paul uttered[5] a deafening cry and lunged[6] at Buddy.

> **Who do Melissa and Buddy mistake for a ghost?**

CHAPTER 10

TR. 10

Melissa screamed, trying to get out of the way. Buddy jumped to his feet and stared down at her.

"Lissa, what's the matter with you?" he shouted.

---

1 **to snuggle against sb.** – *sich an jdn. schmiegen*
2 **practical joke** – *Streich*
3 **to flare** – *funkeln*
4 **twisted** – *gezerrt*
5 **to utter sth.** – *etw. von sich geben*
6 **to lunge at sb.** – *sich auf jdn. stürzen*

Melissa stared up at Paul, who was right behind Buddy.

"Why did you scream like that?" Buddy demanded. "Have you completely lost your mind?"

"Buddy, there he is!" Melissa cried, still on her back on the bed, pointing at Paul.

"Huh?" Buddy turned around. He and Paul were face to face, but Buddy's confused expression didn't change.

"Don't you see him?" Melissa cried. "Didn't you hear him scream at you?"

Buddy turned back to her, looking very worried. "Don't get up," he told her. "Just lie still. I'm going to call your parents."

"Some boyfriend," Paul scoffed[1], now looking. "I'd never treat you like that[2]."

"Paul, make him see you," Melissa pleaded, sitting up.

"No, please, lie still," Buddy urged[3] her.

"I guess he can't see me," Paul said. He put his hand on Buddy's shoulder. Buddy didn't react. "He can't feel me, either." He punched[4] Buddy hard in the back.

"Buddy–watch out!" Melissa screamed, too late.

But Buddy didn't feel a thing.

Paul looked very disappointed.

"Paul, leave him alone!" Melissa cried.

"I-I'll go get Marta," Buddy said, looking panicked.

"Buddy, just listen to me. Stop acting so stupid."

"He can't help it," Paul said, sneering. "He is stupid."

Suddenly Paul started to fade away. First he became transparent[5]. Then he was just a shadowy outline[6]. Then he was gone, leaving behind a rush of cold air.

"Didn't you even feel that?" Melissa asked Buddy.

"Feel what?"

"That cold air."

---

1 **to scoff –** *höhnisch lachen*
2 **I would never treat you like that.–** *So würde ich nie mit dir umgehen.*
3 **to urge sb. to do sth. –** *jdn. drängen, etw. zu tun*
4 **to punch sb. –** *jdn. mit der Faust schlagen*
5 **transparent –** *durchsichtig*
6 **shadowy outline –** *schattiger Umriss*

"It's breezy[1]. Look at the curtains." Buddy replied

"Buddy, I'm not crazy." She climbed to her feet.

"No, of course not," Buddy said. "But maybe you're having some kind of a breakdown[2] or something."

"I don't get it," she said, standing in front of him. "Why can't you just trust[3] me? Paul was right behind you. He screamed at you. He punched you in the back. I'm not hallucinating[4]. It's just that only I can see him."

"Lissa, calm down. This is real life. It isn't some stupid TV sitcom."

"Oh, I see. So now I'm crazy *and* stupid."

"I didn't say that." He put his hands on her shoulders. "Can't you see how worried I am about you?"

"Well, go worry about me at home," she said angrily and backed away.

"You heard me. Go home. I can see that I have to figure out what to do without any help from you."

"But I *do* want to get you help. First we have to tell your parents about this. Then we have to–"

"Go home, Buddy," she said wearily[5].

"Okay. I'll go. If you're sure you'll be okay."

"Yeah. Sure," she said. "I'm going straight to bed, okay?"

"Call me first thing in the morning?"

"Okay." She gave him a weak smile. A few seconds later she heard the front door slam behind him. She sat down on the bed and stared out the window at the round moon.

"Thanks, Paul," she said aloud. "You just cost me a boyfriend."

He appeared at the side of the bed, looking pleased with himself. "So what? You can just buy another one, right?"

"Why do you keep talking about how rich I am all the time?"

"I know you rich girls. You're all alike," he said bitterly. "If I were alive, you wouldn't even look at me."

"How do you know that?" Melissa asked.

---

1 **breezy** – *windig*
2 **breakdown** – *Zusammenbruch*
3 **to trust sb.** – *jdm. trauen*
4 **to hallucinate** – *halluzinieren, Wahnvorstellungen haben*
5 **weary** – *müde, lustlos*

"I know it. You rich people like to stick together." He walked over to the window. The full moon was shining right through his back.

"Buddy isn't rich," she said. "His father works at the post office."

"Then what do you see in Buddy?" Paul asked. "It can't be his great personality." He laughed a dirty laugh.

"Oh, shut up! Why don't you just leave me alone?"

"If you were my girl, I would've been nicer to you," Paul said, ignoring her. Is he jealous[1]? Melissa thought. Is that why he appeared when Buddy was kissing me? A shadow fell over his face. His entire body seemed to be swallowed up[2] by it. Now he was nothing but a dark outline. "I knew you'd break your promise to help me," he said.

"No, Paul. I–"

"I should just kill you now."

The words were a whisper, a whisper in her ear.

"You hit Buddy. He couldn't even feel it. How are you going to kill me?"

"I did that for your benefit[3]," he said, staring at her menacingly. "I was just fooling around[4]. Don't worry. I turned the steering wheel in your precious new car, didn't I? You felt me when I almost pushed you out the window. I managed[5] to open your birthday presents for you."

"Why–why did you do that?"

"You don't listen, do you?" The shadow shifted and floated toward her. "I came back here to kill you. And I will. But not yet. First I want to have some fun. …"

* * *

Melissa thanked the librarian[6] and carried the little roll of microfilm[7] to the viewing booth[8]. It was early Monday morning, and the library was empty except for a man with very thick glasses at a table in the front, leaning over a Wall Street Journal, and a filthy[9], unshaved[10] man snoring[11] loudly in an armchair.

---

1 **jealous** – *eifersüchtig*
2 **to swallow sth. up** – *etw. verschlingen*
3 **for your benefit** – *deinetwegen*
4 **to fool around** – *rumalbern*
5 **to manage to do sth.** – *etw. hinbekommen*
6 **librarian** – *Bibliothekar*
7 **microfilm** – *Mikrofilm*
8 **viewing booth** – *Lesekabine*
9 **filthy** – *dreckig*
10 **unshaven** – *unrasiert*
11 **to snore** – *schnarchen*

I've got to find out the truth about Paul, she thought. Her next thought made her shudder: My life depends on it. And Buddy had let her down, she realized, at a time when she really needed him.

She figured that the death of a local teenager would be front-page news, so she carefully scanned every front page of the Shadyside *Courier* for the past six months. Then, just to be on the safe side[1], she also checked the local news pages and the obituary[2] page.

It took a long time. She was careful not to skip a single day of the entire six months, but she found nothing at all. No story about Paul's death. In fact, she hadn't found a story about a single teenager dying.

Maybe I didn't go back far enough, she thought. Paul said he had died recently. But he didn't remember anything about when it had happened. Maybe he's been dead for years, she thought, yawning. She looked at her watch. It was nearly lunchtime.

She returned the microfilm, stepped past the armchair where the man was still snoring away, and headed[3] out the door. The fresh air and bright sunlight felt so good! She was about to climb in when she saw a familiar face. "Delia! Hi!"

"Got your car back, huh?" Delia called, hurrying up to greet Melissa, a stack of books in her arm.

"How's it running?"

"Great. What are you doing here? I'm so happy to see you."

"Just returning some books," Delia said. "Wait for me?"

Delia returned a few minutes later empty-handed. "So what are you doing here?" she asked.

"It's a weird story," Melissa said, sighing. She wondered if Delia would believe her. Yes. Delia was such a good friend. "Delia, do you remember a boy about our age who died? His name was Paul something."

"Paul Something?" Delia laughed. "I knew a Greg Something and a Mike Something. But Paul–"

"No. Seriously," Melissa said, leaning back against her car.

---

1   **to be on the safe side –** *(ugs.) um auf Nummer sicher zu gehen*
2   **obituary –** *Nachruf, Todesanzeige*
3   **to head –** *sich auf den Weg machen*

"He died?" Delia asked. "I can't think of anyone. Why?"

Melissa had a sudden thought. "You know, maybe he didn't go to Shadyside. He said he was poor and stuff."

"You talked to him?" Delia asked, confused.

"I'll bet[1] he went to South," Melissa said, caught up in her own thoughts. "Yeah. I'll bet he did."

"Well, my cousin Tracy goes to South," Delia said. "Want to see if she's home?"

"Sure," Melissa said. "Do you have anything you have to do right now?"

"Not really," Delia replied and they climbed into the new car. "Tracy lives in the Old Village. I'll direct[2] you."

A short while later Melissa was driving the car through the narrow streets of the Old Village. They found Tracy in her front yard, chasing after[3] two little kids she was baby-sitting. Tracy was short and thin and looked about ten or twelve, even though she was sixteen. She was wearing faded jean cut-offs and a Hard Rock Cafe T-shirt. "Hi!" she called, giving up[4] on catching the two kids.

"Hi, Tracy. You remember Melissa?"

"Yeah. Sure," Tracy said. "The one with the wild hair."

"Well, Melissa wanted to ask you about a boy who went to South," Delia said.

"I mean, maybe he went to South," Melissa said.

"Well, I know most of the kids at South," Tracy said, and then added, "unfortunately."

"Come on, Tracy," Delia said. "South isn't that bad."

"It's a pit[5]," Tracy said, "but why complain? I'm a senior[6] this year. Then I'm out of here!"

"Tracy, do you remember anything about a boy from your school who died this year, or last?" Melissa asked eagerly.

"Huh?"

---

1 **I'll bet ... –** *(ugs.)* Wetten, dass ...
2 **to direct sb. –** *(hier:)* jdn. lotsen
3 **to chase after sb. –** jdm. hinterherrennen
4 **to give up –** aufgeben
5 **pit –** *(ugs.)* Loch
6 **senior –** Oberstufenschüler

"Was there a boy from South about our age who died?"

"Well, yeah. There was," Tracy said, wrinkling her forehead[1]. "There was a boy who died just before school let out[2] last spring."

> How does Melissa start researching Paul's death?

CHAPTER 11

"Now where did I put that old yearbook?" Tracy said, standing on tiptoe[3] to reach the top shelf of her closet. She had put the two kids in the den with a Disney cartoon on the VCR[4]. Then she led Melissa and Delia up to her room to show them a picture of the boy who had died.

"Oh. Here he is. It's not a very good picture. He's standing in the back row. You can only see half his face." Tracy handed the open book to Melissa.

"Where is he? I don't see—"

"Right there," Tracy said, putting her finger on the picture. "The tall, blond guy. His name was Vince. Vince Alexander. Yeah. I remember now. He was a swimmer. Died in a diving[5] accident. His head hit the end of the diving board[6]. Ugh. It was terrible."

Melissa stared at the picture of the smiling boy. Delia put a hand gently on her shoulder. "Lissa, are you okay?"

Melissa silently closed the yearbook. "Yeah. Fine. It's just … he's not the boy."

"Who are you looking for?" Tracy asked, taking the book and tossing it back up on the closet shelf.

"A boy named Paul. I don't know if he went to South."

---

1   **to wrinkle one's forehead** – *die Stirn runzeln*
2   **before school let out** – *vor den Ferien*
3   **on tiptoe** – *auf Zehenspitzen*
4   **VCR** – *Videorekorder*
5   **diving** – *Tauchen*
6   **board** – *Brett*

"Why are you trying to find out about him?" Delia asked

"I … uh … promised someone I would," Melissa said.

Delia gave her a curious[1] look, but Melissa was determined[2] not to say anything more.

They said good-bye to Tracy and drove off. A few minutes later Melissa dropped[3] Delia off, then headed home. The late-afternoon sun was still high in the sky. The road was bubbling[4] in the heat. Shadows from the trees she passed danced on the shiny hood[5]. It all seemed unreal. She had the feeling that she had left the road and was driving high in the sky, on her way to the sun.

"Get real," she said aloud, forcing herself to sit up straight[6]. She pulled down the sun visor and gripped the wheel tighter[7] as if tightening her grip[8] on reality. She concentrated on the curving road, ignoring the glare[9] of the sun and the darting shadows on the car.

I'm not cracking up[10]. I'm not. The ghost is real, she told herself. Paul is real. He lived. He existed. And he died. Sure, the stories about the Fear Street Prowler made me a little jumpy, a little nervous. That's only normal. But if Paul was real, how come she hadn't been able to find out anything about him?

"Paul, are you here?" she asked out loud and waited for a reply. Would she ever be able to go anywhere without wondering if he was invisible[11] at her side, waiting, watching, planning to kill her.

"Paul?" No. He wasn't there.

She pulled into her driveway and stepped out of the car. Shielding[12] her eyes from the sun, she started toward the house but stopped just outside the living-room window.

Someone—just a shadow—was moving about inside.

---

1   **curious** – *neugierig*
2   **determined** – *entschlossen*
3   **to drop sb. off** – *jdn. zu Hause absetzen*
4   **to bubble** – *Blasen werfen*
5   **hood** – *(hier:) Motorhaube*
6   **to sit up straight** – *sich aufrichten*
7   **tighter** – *fester*
8   **grip** – *Griff*
9   **glare** – *grelles Licht*
10 **to crack up** – *(ugs.) durchdrehen*
11 **invisible** – *unsichtbar*
12 **to shield** – *schützen*

Looking at the porch[1], Melissa saw that the front door was wide open. Had someone broken in? She backed away from the window and pressed herself against the wall. Was it the Fear Street Prowler?

She crept back up to the corner of the window and peered[2] inside. The sun on the glass made it hard to see anything. But, yes–someone was in there, a moving shadow among still shadows.

Was it Paul? Had he come downstairs? Was he waiting for her there, waiting for the news she didn't have? A prowler wouldn't walk back and forth[3] like that, would he? Melissa took a deep breath, walked quickly past the window, and headed into the house to see who it was.

> **What did the boy who died at South look like?**

CHAPTER 12

TR. 12

"Buddy!"

He spun around, startled[4] by her cry. "Hi."

"What are you doing here?" she asked, feeling very relieved but remembering how angry she was at him

"Uh … your mom let me in. Then she had to go shopping. Listen, I came to apologize."

"Really?" She sat down on the back of the leather couch and crossed her arms. "You really don't have to–"

"No. I want to. I mean … well, I mean I'm sorry. That's all." He took a few steps toward her.

---

1 **porch –** *Veranda*
2 **to peer –** *spähen*
3 **back and forth –** *rauf und runter*
4 **startled –** *überrumpelt*

"Buddy, you still don't believe me about Paul," she said, tugging at the silver pendant on her neck.

"Lissa, please–let's not start up with that."

"But if you don't, if you just think I'm crazy–"

"I don't think you're crazy," he protested[1], putting his hands in his shorts pockets. "Listen, I had an idea. Let's just go out tonight and have some fun. What do you say?"

She looked at him doubtfully. "Fun?"

"Yeah. I'll pick you up about eight. We'll go to Red Heat."

"Well …"

"Come on, Lissa. You've always wanted to go there."

Melissa smiled and uncrossed her arms. Buddy really was trying to be nice. He hated loud, crowded[2] dance clubs. He had always refused to take her to Red Heat in the past.

"Okay. Great!" she said. She walked over to him and kissed him on the cheek. "You are forgiven[3]".

He grinned back at her. "That was easy. What would you have done if I'd asked you out for dinner[4] too?"

"I'm not that kind of girl," she replied.

Before it had become a teen dance club, Red Heat had been a farm equipment warehouse[5]. From the outside, the long, tall building still looked like one. But as soon as they stepped onto the hangar-size dance floor, they forgot that.

It had been covered with colored flooring–pink, black and orange squares on pale green, all clashing[6]. When the flashing lights hit the dance floor, it seemed to come to life, and the warehouse became a different world. The walls had all been painted red, although it wasn't bright enough to see the true color. The long bar[7] and all of the other furnishings were red, in

---

1 **to protest –** *widersprechen*
2 **crowded –** *voll (mit Menschen)*
3 **You are forgiven. –** *Es sei dir verziehen.*
4 **to ask sb. out for dinner –** *jdn. auf ein Abendessen einladen*
5 **warehouse –** *Lagerhaus*
6 **clashing colors –** *Farben, die sich beißen*
7 **bar –** *Theke*

keeping with[1] the name Red Heat. Giant black speakers blasted[2] the music down to the floor, which shook from the booming sound, holding the dancers as if in a powerful spell[3].

"I guess they call it Red Heat because it's eight hundred degrees in here!" Buddy shouted, dripping with sweat. "What?" Melissa, holding on to his shoulders, leaned closer to hear what he was saying over the music.

They had been dancing for nearly an hour and Melissa, wearing a sparkly top[4] and a purple skirt, felt great–dizzy[5] and exhausted[6]. It felt so good not to think about anything, just to move mindlessly[7] to the music. She hadn't thought about the ghost once. Where was he, anyway?

She had called to him in her room after dinner. But he hadn't replied. And there was no sign of him, no cold wind, no whisper, no shadows across the carpet.

"I haven't seen the ghost all day," she told Buddy, thinking about her morning in the library.

"What?" He pulled her off the dance floor, toward the red bar against the far wall. "I need something to drink."

"Me too. A Coke or something." The music was pounding on all sides. Red and green lights played against their faces, making them look unreal[8].

"What did you say?" Buddy asked, shouting to be heard.

"Just a Coke or something."

"No. Before that."

"I said I hadn't seen Paul all day."

"I thought we weren't going to talk about that," Buddy said sharply.

"I wasn't. I mean …" She grabbed his arm. "Buddy, it's hard not to think about him. He's threatened[9] to kill me."

"What?"

---

1 **in keeping with –** *passend zu*
2 **to blast music –** *Musik rausdröhnen*
3 **in a powerful spell –** *unter einem mächtigen Bann*
4 **sparkly top –** *glitzerndes Oberteil*
5 **dizzy –** *schwindelig*
6 **exhausted –** *erschöpft*
7 **mindless –** *(hier:) geistesabwesend*
8 **unreal –** *irreal, unwirklich*
9 **to threaten to do sth. –** *damit drohen, etw. zu tun*

"You heard me. I told you the whole story. He thinks I killed him and unless I find out who really did it, he's going to–"
"Melissa!" He shouted angrily. "Stop–please!"
She let go of his arm. "I can't stop because it's real. It's happening to me, Buddy. And I can't stop thinking about it. You're just going to have to believe me, and–"
He pulled away, his face red, then green, then red again, looking very upset.
"No. Stop. I can't believe it. I just can't. You're going to spoil[1] the whole night, Lissa!"
"No, I'm not!" she screamed. "You already have!"
She turned and started to run, bumping into a surprised couple[2]. She made her way quickly across the crowded dance floor, surrounded by the throbbing[3] music, her heart pounding along with it, running through the flashing colors. At the end of the dance floor, she turned back to see if Buddy was following her. She felt angry, disappointed–and relieved–when she couldn't see him. Melissa pushed the heavy glass door, and escaped[4] into the night.

It was a warm night, but the air felt cold against her skin. Breathing loudly, she ran across the gravel[5] toward the parking lot[6].
Where was she going?
She didn't know. She didn't even think about it. She was so angry, so hurt. Buddy just wanted her to be cheerful and pretend[7] everything was okay. He wasn't the least bit[8] interested in her problem, in her *very real* problem. Buddy really thought she was crazy. As long as she kept it to herself[9], he was happy. He didn't care what happened to her. As long as she shut up about it[10].

---

1 **to spoil sth.** – *etw. vermasseln*
2 **couple** – *Pärchen*
3 **throbbing** – *pulsierend*
4 **to escape** – *fliehen, entkommen*
5 **gravel** – *Kies, Schotter*
6 **parking lot** – *Parkplatz*
7 **to pretend** – *so tun, als ob*
8 **the least bit** – *im Geringsten*
9 **to keep sth. to oneself** – *etw. für sich behalten*
10 **to shut up about sth.** – *etw. verschweigen*

She stumbled on the gravel and suddenly realized she had run halfway across the vast parking lot. She was surrounded by rows[1] of cars. She turned back toward the club. The sound of laughter made her turn around.

Some boys were sitting on car hoods at the dark edge of the lot. There were four or five of them, wearing blue denim jeans and black leather or denim jackets. They were leaning back on the car hoods, joking around, drinking beer from cans[2].

Their laughter was loud and cruel[3]. They had obviously been drinking for a while. I'll head back toward the club, she thought. I don't think they've even noticed me yet.

She took a step back, trying to hide in the car shadows. One of them called to her. "Hey–how you doin'?" He raised his beer and grinned.

"Don't go!" another one yelled[4]. "Join the party!"

Melissa shook her head, backing away. Two of the boys, both sitting on the low hood of a yellow Camaro, got into a playful shoving match[5]. "You ask her," one of them said.

"No. You ask her."

The one on the left gave his friend a hard shove, and the laughing boy, his beer can flying up in the air, fell off the car and rolled across the gravel to Melissa's feet.

"Hey, foxy[6]–" he started.

Uncertain of what to do, Melissa looked down at his grinning face. And then her mouth fell open in surprise. Even in the dim, gray light in this darkest part of the parking lot, she recognized[7] him at once.

"Paul–what are you *doing* here?" she asked.

> **Why does Melissa leave Buddy and run out of the club?**

---

1 **row –** *Reihe*
2 **can –** *Dose*
3 **cruel –** *böse*
4 **to yell –** *brüllen*
5 **They got into a playful shoving match. –** *Sie begannen, sich gegenseitig aus Spaß zu schubsen.*
6 **foxy –** *sexy*
7 **to recognize sb. –** *jdn. wiedererkennen*

He stared up at her without getting up. The wide, foolish[1] grin seemed to be stuck[2] to his face.

"Hey–do I know you?" he asked.

His friends laughed..

"Paul–" she started, her heart pounding, her throat suddenly dry.

"That's my name. Don't wear it out."

Again, laughter from his friends. One of them walked over, a similar foolish grin on his face, bent down, and pulled Paul to his feet. The two of them stood unsteadily[3], staring at Melissa, looking her up and down.

Melissa was so startled to see Paul there in that dark parking lot with his loud, drunken friends that she forgot her fear. "You–you can see him?" she asked the boy who had pulled Paul to his feet.

They all laughed again and climbed down from their car hoods. They were coming towards her slowly, sipping from their cans as they walked.

"You really can see him?" Melissa repeated.

"Not if I see him first!" Paul joked and dropped back down to his knees, laughing. It was obvious that he'd had too much to drink.

"But … you're real!" Melissa stammered[4].

This got a big reaction from all of them. They hooted and howled[5]. Turning quickly, Melissa saw that they had formed a circle around her. I'm trapped, she thought, feeling a rush of panic. They're closing in on me[6].

"Yeah, I'm real," Paul said quietly, turning serious. "Want me to prove it?" He grabbed her arm.

"Let go of me!" Melissa shouted, forcing[7] herself to sound more angry than afraid.

---

1 **foolish –** *albern*
2 **stuck –** *geklebt*
3 **unsteady –** *schwankend*
4 **to stammer –** *stottern*
5 **to hoot and howl –** *vor Lachen heulen*
6 **to close in on sb. –** *sich auf jdn. zubewegen*
7 **to force oneself to do sth. –** *sich dazu zwingen, etw. zu tun*

To her surprise, he quickly let go. "Hey–you were coming on to me[1], weren't you?" he said accusingly[2].

"No. I wasn't," Melissa protested, trying to figure out how to get away from these boys and get back to Buddy. Why hadn't Buddy come looking for her? Didn't he care at all?

"You're just a tease[3], huh?" Paul said, sneering.

"Paul, why are you doing this?" she asked. "Why are you acting so … different?"

He glared[4] at her. "Huh?"

"Yeah, Paul. Why are you acting so different?" One of Paul's friends mimicked[5] Melissa. The boy stepped forward and grabbed Melissa's shoulder. "What do you see in him[6], anyway?"

"Hey–leave her alone," Paul said, his face suddenly turning ugly. He gave his friend a hard shove. The boy fell back against a car. "She wants me–not you," Paul said.

The boy got up quickly. "Oh, yeah? How about we let her decide, okay?"

"She's already decided," Paul said, his hands curling into tight fists at his sides.

"Stop it! Just stop it!" Melissa shouted, frightened and confused. How come his friends could see Paul so clearly? Was it possible that he wasn't a ghost after all? That he had somehow managed to trick[7] her back in her room? "Let me go!" she shouted.

"What's the matter?" Paul scoffed. "You too good for us?"

"I want to go now," Melissa said slowly, pronouncing[8] each word distinctly[9]. She didn't want them to know how frightened she was. Her knees were shaking.

"Let her go," the boy Paul had shoved said quietly.

"Don't tell me what to do!" Paul screamed, turning on his friend. "Don't ever tell me what to do!"

---

1 **to come on to sb.** – *jdn. anmachen*
2 **accusing** – *anklagend, beschuldigend*
3 **You're just a tease.** – *Du schäkerst nur gerne.*
4 **to glare at sb.** – *jdn. wütend anfunkeln*
5 **to mimic** – *jdn. nachäffen*
6 **What do you see in him?** – *Was gefällt dir an ihm?*
7 **to trick sb.** – *jdn. täuschen*
8 **to pronounce** – *aussprechen*
9 **distinct** – *verschieden, eindeutig*

"I just said, let her go," the boy replied.

"I'll let her go when I'm finished with her," Paul said, his voice turning low and threatening. And without any further warning[1], he lunged at his friend, grabbing his shoulders, and the two of them fell to the gravel, rolling around, wrestling hard and furiously[2], screaming at each other as the others gleefully[3] looked on.

Melissa began running back across the parking lot toward the club.

"Hey—come back here!" She recognized Paul's angry voice and kept running. The rows of cars on both sides of her seemed endless. She heard them coming after her, tried to pick up speed, and nearly lost her balance[4] on the gravel. The lights were out in that section of the parking lot, and the sudden darkness frightened her even more.

They're catching up[5], she realized.

"Hey, Blondie, we just want to have some fun!" one of them yelled. The others laughed and kept chasing her.

Several couples were watching them in the parking lot. Because of all the laughter, they must have thought it was all a joke. The entrance to the club came into view. Would she be safe inside? Yes. They wouldn't follow her in there.

"Hey, Blondie, we won't hurt you! Honest!"

Why did Paul act so weird, so cold, so horrible? She had spent most of the day trying to help him, trying to find out what really happened to him. Now here he was, acting so gross[6], like a complete animal, as if he didn't know her at all. Was he just showing off[7] for his buddies[8]?

Out of breath, her heart pounding, but almost at the door, she turned back and saw that Paul and his friends were no longer chasing her. In fact, they were gone.

Shadows slid[9] through the long rows of cars. When did they stop chasing her? And where did they go? The club doors opened and music burst out

---

1   **without further warning –** *ohne weitere Warnung*
2   **furious –** *wütend*
3   **gleeful –** *fröhlich*
4   **to lose one's balance –** *das Gleichgewicht verlieren*
5   **to catch up –** *aufholen*
6   **gross –** *eklig*
7   **to show off –** *prahlen*
8   **buddy –** *Kumpel*
9   **to slide –** *gleiten*

into the silence, startling her. Then they shut. The parking lot fell silent[1] again. Still shielding her eyes, Melissa stared out at the rows of cars. Where did Paul and his friends go? How did they disappear so quickly?

Were they all ghosts?

A hand touched her shoulder.

"No!" she screamed and backed away.

"Hey Melissa, what's wrong?" Buddy asked, concerned, flashing red, then black, then red again under the spotlight.

"Buddy, please, take me home," she said. She grabbed his arm. He felt so solid, so real.

"I couldn't find you," he said. "I didn't know you were outside."

"I'm sorry—" she started. She heard a noise somewhere down the nearest row of cars. Paul and his friends?

Buddy followed her gaze. "Melissa, what is it?"

"I–I thought I saw something."

"It's too dark down there. Some of the lights are out."

She held on to him tightly. They were both flashing red, then black, red, then black, as if they were materializing[2] and then disappearing like ghosts.

"Melissa, you're shaking all over."

"I'm just … tired, I guess." She wasn't going to tell him that she saw Paul in the parking lot. Paul and his ghost friends. Paul and his real friends. She knew if she told Buddy, they'd just start to argue[3] again. He'd get that worried look on his face and say they should tell her parents immediately.

"Sorry I'm such a downer[4]. Please take me home."

He put his arm around her shoulders and led her to the car. Melissa walked quickly, alert[5] to any sound or sign that Paul and his friends were there, hiding, watching, waiting.

But they had disappeared into thin air.

She slid into the passenger seat and closed her eyes. Buddy talked excitedly about what a great club Red Heat was, and what a great sound system they

---

1 **to fall silent –** *still werden*
2 **to materialize –** *sich materialisieren*
3 **to argue –** *sich streiten*
4 **Sorry I'm such a downer. –** *Tut mir leid, ich bin so eine Spaßbremse.*
5 **alert –** *wachsam*

had, and how they should go there more often, but that it was so expensive. He had obviously decided to forget the fact that they had had an argument. Maybe Buddy thought that if he ignored the whole thing, Paul would just go away. Melissa wished Buddy was right. If only Paul would go away…

An hour later, in bed, Melissa couldn't get to sleep. When she closed her eyes, she saw Paul and his friends shoving one another against the cars and drinking from cans; she saw them circling around[1] her and closing in on her. She couldn't get Paul's face out of her mind, his cruel laughter, the way he threatened her, the way he grabbed her so fiercely[2], the way he looked at her. The way he hated her. Yes. That was what Melissa found so frightening: Paul *hated* her. It was a warm, humid night, but the bedroom window was closed and locked[3]. The streetlight down below cast a pale yellow light onto the ceiling. I've never been hated before, Melissa thought. Sure, there had been kids she didn't get along with. But she had never been hated so blindly, so heatedly. Never. He really has come back to kill me, she thought.

Somehow she had never taken his threat seriously[4]. She had thought she could reason[5] with him, help him. He had seemed jealous of Buddy, after all. And because of that, Melissa had even fooled[6] herself into thinking that maybe Paul wasn't so bad after all.

But seeing him there on that dark parking lot with his friends, seeing how hard he was, how bitter, how cruel, she realized that she was wrong about him. He would never be her friend. He could kill her. He meant what he said. He hated her that much.

She sat straight up when she felt the rush of cold air. A few seconds later Paul appeared, first a dark outline in front of the window, then a shadowy form moving quickly to the foot of the bed. Melissa couldn't see his face. It was covered in shadow. He was still wearing the straight-legged blue jeans and the denim jacket.

"Get out of here!" she screamed, gripping the covers. The ghost seemed to float up until he was above her, his dark eyes staring coldly down at her.

---

1 **to circle around sb. –** *um jdn. kreisen*
2 **fierce –** *heftig, scharf, wild*
3 **to lock –** *abschließen*
4 **to take sth. seriously –** *etw. ernst nehmen*
5 **to reason with sb. –** *mit jdm. (vernünftig) reden*
6 **to fool oneself into thinking that… –** *sich vormachen, dass…*

"Get out!" Melissa repeated, feeling his eyes burn into hers. "Just go away!"
The ghost began to fade. The eyes dimmed[1], the face darkened, the floating form became a dim outline.
"I'll be back. I'm not finished here," Paul said, words more chilling than the air he left behind.

How does Buddy behave on the way back from the club?

CHAPTER 14

TR. 14

"No, I can't, Delia. Not this morning anyway."
Melissa opened the curtains and looked out the bedroom window. It was a gray day, dark clouds covered the sky.
"Yeah. Buddy and I had a pretty good time last night." She didn't feel like getting into it with Delia first thing in the morning. She realized she hadn't confided[2] at all in her best friend. She wanted to tell her about Paul. She needed to. Delia would probably believe her, and Melissa desperately needed someone to believe her.
I'll tell her all about it when my parents are away, when I stay at her house this weekend, Melissa thought.
They chatted for a few more minutes. Then Melissa promised to call her later and went down to breakfast. She found her mother at the table with the morning paper and a half-eaten dry English muffin. Her father, leaning on the kitchen counter[3], was having a heated[4] telephone discussion with someone about plane reservations.
"Morning," Mrs. Dryden muttered from behind her paper.

---

1 **to dim –** *dunkler werden, verlöschen*
2 **to confide in sb. –** *sich jdm. anvertrauen*
3 **kitchen counter –** *Küchenarbeitsplatte*
4 **heated –** *hitzig, erregt*

"Who's Daddy talking to?" Melissa asked, getting herself a bowl of corn flakes.

"Travel agent," her mother said, chewing the dry, toasted muffin. "Some problem with our tickets to Las Vegas. He's going in late today." She lowered the paper and stared at Melissa. "Look at the rings under your eyes."

"Mother, that's physically impossible. You can't look at your own eyes."

"Didn't you sleep?"

"Not too well," Melissa admitted.

"I'm not interested in your problems." Mr. Dryden's voice boomed[1] into the phone. "You have to get us boarding passes[2] with our tickets. I know how airlines overbook[3] these days."

"Poor Daddy," Melissa said, her mouth full of corn flakes.

"I really think you should change your mind," her mother said.

"What?"

"You know. Come to the convention with us. It'll do you good to get away. You've had such a boring summer."

Melissa laughed. "Believe me, it hasn't been boring."

Her mother looked disappointed. "You won't come?"

"No. Really. I don't think so."

Melissa pretended to concentrate on her corn flakes. Running away to Las Vegas, she knew, wouldn't help her. She had to find out the truth about Paul, find out what really happened to him. It was the only way she could get rid of him, the only way he would leave her alone.

Melissa ate quickly, pushed her chair away from the table, and waving to her father, headed toward the front door. "Where are you off to?" Mrs. Dryden called after her.

"Just meeting Delia," Melissa lied.

The sky looked a little less threatening as she backed[4] her car down the drive. The clouds had lifted. Melissa turned down The Mill Road and headed toward town. The dashboard clock read 11:58. How had she slept so late?

---

1 **to boom** – *posaunen*
2 **boarding pass** – *Bordkarte*
3 **to overbook** – *überbuchen*
4 **to back a car** – *rückwärts fahren*

She turned into the large Shop 'N' Stop parking lot on Division Street and started looking for a parking space[1]. Maybe today won't be a total waste of time like yesterday, she thought. Maybe today I'll find some answers about Paul.

The night before, Melissa had recognized one of the boys in the parking lot from somewhere. His name was Frankie. Then it came to her in the middle of the night: he delivered groceries for the Shop 'N' Stop.

The parking lot was completely full, so Melissa had to park on the street outside. She climbed out, locked the car, and crossed the lot. She started to feel nervous.

Frankie, she had noticed, had hung back the night before. He hadn't threatened her or stood in her way. In fact, he had seemed a little embarrassed[2] by the whole thing.

And, she told herself, talking to him while he's at work is perfectly safe. He's not going to try anything[3] in the middle of the supermarket. Frankie was her only clue[4] now, the only person she knew who actually could tell her about Paul.

The doors opened. Melissa stepped into the cold air of the vast[5] supermarket – and was surprised to see Frankie without having to search for him. He was at the end of the nearest checkout line[6], bagging groceries[7] for a young woman with a baby in a carrier on her back. Melissa hesitated, wondering what she was going to say to him. Maybe this is a stupid idea, she thought. Frankie looked up, having packed the last of the groceries, and saw her. At first he seemed confused, as if he didn't remember who she was. Then suddenly a broad smile of recognition[8] spread over his face.

As Melissa walked up to him, the smile faded, replaced by a wary[9] look.

"Frankie?" she asked uncertainly.

---

1 **parking space** – *Parkplatz*
2 **to be embarrassed by sth.** – *etw. peinlich finden*
3 **to try something** – *(ugs.) sich daneben verhalten*
4 **clue** – *Hinweis*
5 **vast** – *gewaltig, gigantisch*
6 **checkout line** – *Schlange an der Kasse*
7 **to bag groceries** – *Einkäufe eintüten*
8 **recognition** – *Wiedererkennung*
9 **wary** – *vorsichtig*

"Hey, look–I don't want no trouble," he said. His straight brown hair was tied behind his head in a short ponytail. He was wearing a long white Shop 'N' Stop apron over black jeans and a crisp blue work shirt.

"No, I–" Melissa started.

"I didn't do nothing last night. The other guys– I didn't think they should've …" His voice trailed off[1]. He was looking past Melissa to a large woman behind a counter[2], probably his supervisor[3].

"I didn't come because of last night. I want to ask you about something else."

He shook his head, straightening the stack of grocery bags.

"It'll only take a minute. I promise," Melissa pleaded.

He hesitated. "Well, okay. I'll take my break now." He walked over and said something to the woman behind the counter, then motioned[4] for Melissa to follow him.

She followed him down a long aisle[5] to a large storeroom[6] against the back wall. It was even colder in this room and smelled of rotting[7] fruits and vegetables.

Frankie pulled down a wooden crate[8]. Melissa lowered herself onto the crate and crossed her legs[9]. He continued to stand. "I only get ten minutes for my break."

"I want to ask you about Paul."

Frankie smiled. "You really got the hots[10] for Paul, huh?"

Melissa could feel herself blushing[11]. "No. That's not why … I mean … Listen, you and Paul were friends?"

"Yeah. We're buddies[12]. Paul's a pretty bad dude[13]."

---

1 **to trail off** – *verstummen*
2 **counter** – *Theke*
3 **supervisor** – *Leiter*
4 **to motion** – *bedeuten*
5 **aisle** – *Gang*
6 **storeroom** – *Lagerraum*
7 **to rot** – *verfaulen*
8 **wooden crate** – *Holzkiste*
9 **to cross one's legs** – *die Beine übereinanderschlagen*
10 **to have the hots for sb.** – *in jdn. verknallt sein*
11 **to blush** – *erröten, rot werden*
12 **to be buddies** – *befreundet sein*
13 **dude** – *Typ*

"What do you mean by bad?" she asked uncomfortably, suddenly wishing she hadn't come here.

"I mean, he's my buddy, but I don't go along with some things[1]... I mean, I don't know anything at all. Really."

Frankie looked up at the clock above the storeroom door. Melissa realized she'd better get to the point. "When did Paul die?" she asked.

Frankie's mouth dropped open. He pulled at his ponytail. "Huh?"

"Paul. You know. When did he die? Can you tell me—"

"Paul's dead?" He sat down on the floor next to Melissa. "When? Last night? No. No. Wait That's impossible. I talked to him on the phone this morning. Before work."

Now Melissa was completely confused. "Maybe we're talking about different Pauls," she said.

"Yeah. Maybe." Frankie still looked very upset.

"The Paul I'm talking about died some time ago," Melissa said.

Frankie stood back up. "Hey—you really scared me."

"I-I'm sorry," Melissa stammered. "But I wanted to ask—"

Frankie looked up at the clock again. "Hey, sorry, but I gotta get back to work and I need a soda[2] first. If I'm late after a break, I'll be busted[3]." He turned and hurried from the storeroom.

The swinging doors closed behind him. Melissa sat on the crate for a few minutes trying to make sense[4] of what he had just told her. But it didn't make sense.

They were talking about the same Paul. That was the only thing Melissa was certain of. But was Paul dead or alive, a living, breathing human or a ghost? She knew that Paul was a ghost. He had told her he was a ghost. He appeared and disappeared like a ghost. So how could Frankie not realize that his buddy was dead? How could he have talked to Paul before going to work?

As she walked past him to the exit, Frankie looked up from the bag he was packing and gave her a curious look.

---

1 **I don't go along with some things.** – *In manchen Dingen bin ich nicht der gleichen Meinung.*
2 **soda** – *Limonde*
3 **to be busted** – *Riesenärger bekommen*
4 **to make sense of sth.** – *etw. zusammenreimen*

He thinks I'm crazy, Melissa thought.

Maybe I am.

Stepping outside the supermarket, she saw that the pavement was wet. It must have rained while she was inside, and now the sky was clearing, sunlight sparkling off the wet cars in the parking lot.

She walked around a large puddle and headed for her car.

She heard footsteps behind her, but didn't think anything of them. A car trunk[1] slammed shut. A baby was crying back by the supermarket. She heard the footsteps again as she turned a corner and headed down the last row of cars. They sounded closer behind her now. She turned around, just to see who it was–and saw a flash of color as someone ducked[2] behind a car. Was she seeing things[3]?

She turned and started walking again, a little faster. She took several steps, then spun around again. Again, a flash of dark color. A dark blue jacket maybe. Dark hair. Someone's following me. That was her first thought.

It looks like Paul. That was her second.

But why would Paul hide behind a car? He could appear and disappear. He didn't have to hide. Should she stop and wait for him?

No. She could feel the fear creeping up her body, catching at her throat. No. She decided to run.

She turned and began running to the street. He isn't following me–is he? But he was. The footsteps, scraping against the pavement, splashing through the puddles[4]. Right behind her now. What was the point of running? She stopped and turned. "Paul!"

He grabbed her shoulder.

Why does Melissa drive to the supermarket?

---

1   **trunk –** *Kofferraum*
2   **to duck –** *sich ducken*
3   **to see things –** *Visionen haben*
4   **to splash in a puddle –** *in eine Pfütze treten*

CHAPTER 15

He grinned at her, a hard, cold grin, not friendly, not amused. His grip on her shoulder tightened[1].

"Paul, why—"

"You missed me, huh?"

"What? What do you mean?"

"I heard you calling me back there."

"Let go, Paul. You're hurting me."

He slowly let go. He was standing close to her, too close. He pressed his face close to her cheek. She could feel his breath, hot against her skin.

Feel his breath?

Do ghosts breathe?

Frightened, she took a step back, but he moved forward.

"Why'd you run away last night?" he asked, his dark, cold eyes staring into hers. "You and me could be good together."

"You were so awful," she said. "And those disgusting friends of yours."

"Hey—they're my buddies." He seemed amused by her reaction to them. "They're good guys."

"What do you want, Paul?" She took another step back and backed into the trunk of a big Oldsmobile. He moved forward. If he took one more step, she'd be pinned against the trunk.

"What does any red-blooded[2] American boy want from a nice-looking girl?" He laughed

"Get away from me. Why are you acting like this?"

He looked hurt[3]. "Listen, you came on to me last night."

"I did not. And why are you acting like such a creep? I've been trying to help you."

"Huh?"

"Like I promised."

---

1 **to tighten –** *fester werden*
2 **red-blooded –** *heißblütig*
3 **hurt –** *beleidigt*

"Huh?" He looked confused, then unbuttoned his denim jacket, revealing a blue, sleeveless[1] t-shirt underneath. "You want to help me?" He gave her a dirty grin.

She shoved him and pulled away[2] from the trunk, running hard between cars to get to her car on the street.

"Hey–" he called, trotting after her. "Don't run away again. I thought you wanted to help me."

"Just go away!" she shouted.

"Now you're hurting my feelings," he called. "I don't like it when rich, snobby girls hurt my feelings."

He's crazy, she thought. I've got to get away from him. She reached her car, pulled the door handle. She forgot she had locked it. She plunged[3] her hand into her bag and began frantically rummaging around[4] for her keys. But now he had caught up to her. Smiling triumphantly[5], he grabbed her bag and held it away from her.

"Give it back," she demanded, reaching for it and missing.

"Come and get it!" he said again.

"Paul!" She tried to grab it, but he twirled[6] away, keeping it away from her.

"Give it back–now! You're not funny!"

He didn't give back the bag, and his smile faded. "You're not gonna give me a chance, are you?" he said.

"What?"

"You heard me."

"I don't know what you're talking about. Just give me back my bag."

"I'm not a bad guy. Really. But you'd never want to find that out."

"Paul, you're talking crazy. Please give me back my bag. I've got to go." She made another wild grab[7] for the bag. He pulled it away and put it under his arm.

"Paul–come on!" she cried.

---

1   **sleeveless** – *ärmellos*
2   **to pull away** – *abrücken*
3   **to plunge** – *eintauchen*
4   **to rummage around** – *durchstöbern*
5   **triumphantly** – *triumphierend, selbstgefällig*
6   **to twirl** – *wirbeln*
7   **She made another wild grab for the bag.** – *Sie griff noch einmal wild nach der Tasche.*

"How did you know my name?" he demanded.

"What? You told it to me."

"I didn't. Come on. Tell me. How d'you know my name?"

"Paul, don't be ridiculous—"

She saw the police car before he did. The black-and-white car pulled up beside them. The officer on the passenger looked out the window.

"This your car?" he asked Melissa.

She nodded, glancing at Paul, who gave her back her bag immediately and stood looking suddenly very pale[1].

"Well, it's in a No Parking zone. What's your name? Can I see your driver's license[2]?"

"Melissa Dryden," she said searching in her bag for her wallet. "I didn't see the sign. I didn't realize …"

Suddenly, the other policeman shouted, "Forget it, Ernie. We've got an emergency call[3]. Let's roll!"

The blaring siren[4] starting up made Melissa jump.

"Hey," Paul said, visibly[5] relieved. "You got a break[6] there, huh? I'd never get a break like that. That's for sure."

"Bye!" She opened the car and slid behind the wheel.

"Whoa. Wait, Melissa, I—uh—I'm sorry I gave you a hard time[7]," he said, looking apologetic[8]. "I was just having a little fun. I didn't mean—"

She slammed the car door and missed the rest of what he had to say. She pulled away, leaving him on the curb[9],

watching him in the mirror, expecting him to disappear into thin air. But he didn't move.

I've got to get rid[10] of him, she thought, speeding through a yellow light[11], then making a sharp left turn. He's taking over my life. A few minutes later

---

1 **pale** – *blass*
2 **driver's license** – *Führerschein*
3 **emergency call** – *Notruf*
4 **blaring siren** – *Martinshorn*
5 **visibly** – *sichtbar*
6 **to get a break** – *es leicht haben*
7 **to give sb. a hard time** – *jdm. zusetzen*
8 **apologetic** – *entschuldigend, unterwürfig*
9 **curb** – *Bordsteinkante*
10 **to get rid of sb.** – *jdn. loswerden*
11 **to speed through a light** – *über eine Ampel rasen*

she parked the car in the drive, ran into the house, shouted hello to Marta, who was vacuuming the living room, and ran up to her room.

"No!" she shouted.

Paul, sitting on her bed, stood up quickly.

"No! Stop following me! Just leave me alone!"

Ignoring her pleas, he moved toward her quickly, his dark eyes aglow.

Why do the police stop and talk to Melissa?

CHAPTER 16

TR. 16

She stepped back toward the hallway. He stopped in the center of the room. The strong sunlight from the bedroom window seemed to shine right through him. His dark hair, his denim jacket, his jeans were all outlined in gold.

"Hey, what's happening?" he asked.

Melissa didn't reply. She waited to see if he'd come closer.

"Why are you so scared of me all of a sudden?" he asked, looking suspicious[1].

"Don't play dumb,[2]" Melissa said, her arms crossed protectively[3] in front of her.

"I'm losing control," he said softly, and as he spoke he started to fade, making the sunlight from the window seem brighter. "I keep fading in and out."

"You were solid enough in the parking lot," Melissa said angrily.

---

1   **suspicious –** (hier:) misstrauisch
2   **to play dumb –** sich dumm stellen
3   **protective –** schützend

"Huh?" The shimmering[1] stopped and he stood solidly on the carpet again. For the first time, Melissa realized, he looked frightened. Behind the anger and bitterness[2], he was just a frightened teenager.

"How'd you get back here so quickly?" she asked. The sunlight was making it hard to see him. She walked around him, keeping her distance[3], and sat down on the windowsill, her back to the sun.

"Get back? What are you talking about?"

"I left you standing outside the parking lot. Now here you are," she said. The sun felt good on her back.

He shook his head. "You've totally lost it."

"You've totally lost it," Melissa told him. "Not me."

"I've been here all morning," he said. "Sort of drifting in and out."

"Come on, Paul, you were at the supermarket."

He shook his head. "No. It wasn't me."

"You grabbed my bag and wouldn't give it back."

He moved his hand up to her desk lamp. His hand went through the lamp. "I can't grab anything today," he said with real sadness. "I couldn't grab your bag if I wanted to." His whole body seemed to fade, as if the effort[4] of talking was too much for him. He looked so sad, so frightened now. Melissa thought: is he just trying to throw me off guard[5] for some reason?

"I suppose it wasn't you last night," she said.

He looked surprised. "Last night? When I appeared here last night, you screamed and told me to leave you alone."

"No, I meant before that," Melissa said impatiently. "At the dance club."

"That wasn't me either. Someone who looked like me, maybe."

She refused to believe him. "It was you, Paul. It wasn't a look-alike. You mean you don't remember?"

"I remember last night. I went out, trying to find my old neighborhood[6]. But I didn't find it, so I came back here."

---

1 **shimmer –** *Schimmer*
2 **bitterness –** *Verbitterung, Groll*
3 **to keep one's distance –** *einen Abstand einhalten*
4 **effort –** *Anstrengung*
5 **to throw sb. off guard –** *jemanden unvorbereitet treffen*
6 **my old neighborhood –** *mein altes Viertel*

"You're putting me on, right? You were with your buddies at the cars, drinking beers, and when I came out, you—"

"My buddies? What buddies?"

"I don't know their names. Frankie was one of them."

"Frankie?" A smile slowly crossed his face. "Yeah. Frankie. Hey—I remember him. Frankie Marcuso. Yeah. He was my neighbor. Great guy. Wow. I'd forgotten all about him. Who else was there?"

His whole face brightened when I mentioned his friend, Melissa thought. I've been so scared of him, too scared to realize how lonely[1] and frightened he is.

"I don't know your friends. They were creeps."

"Hey, wait a minute." He floated to his feet. "Don't put my buddies down[2]."

"Listen, is this some kind of joke or something?" Melissa asked, leaning back against the windowsill.

"No. No joke," he said quietly, looking away from her.

"Then we have to figure this out," Melissa said. "Don't you see? You were in two places at once, Paul. Right?"

He looked very confused, pacing[3] rapidly back and forth. "Yeah. I guess so. So what does it mean?"

Melissa looked down at the floor, thinking hard. The Paul at the dance club and at the parking lot had seemed so much more solid, so much angrier, so much more—alive!

Alive!

She stared at the ghost, floating so lightly, so soundlessly[4] back and forth across the carpet. And she had an idea.

"Paul, I think I know."

He stopped pacing. "I think I know too." He stared at her angrily. "This is all a trick, isn't it? To stall for time.[5]"

"Paul, just listen to me. I think maybe I've figured out what's happening. We just assumed you were a ghost from the past," she said.

---

1 **lonely –** *einsam*
2 **to put sb. down –** *schlecht von jdm. reden*
3 **to pace –** *schreiten*
4 **soundless –** *klanglos, still*
5 **To stall for time. –** *Um Zeit zu gewinnen.*

"Huh? What do you mean?"

"We assumed that you died some time ago. You died in the past[1], and you've come from the past to the present to avenge[2] your death."

"Yeah, well, of course," he said, obviously confused.

"Well, maybe we were wrong," Melissa said. "What if you are a ghost from the future?"

"What? You mean like some stupid science-fiction movie or something?"

"No. Not that. Just think a minute. What if you haven't died yet? What if you're still alive?" As she said it, it all became clearer to Melissa. She knew she was right. She had to be right.

"You mean–"

"I mean you're a ghost from the future, Paul. You haven't died yet. You've come back in time."

"It doesn't make any sense," he said, scowling. "I told you, you've totally lost it."

"Just think about it!" Melissa cried, too excited to get exasperated with him. "The Paul I saw at the dance club last night, the Paul with all his buddies– he was still alive. And the Paul who followed me at the supermarket parking lot this morning–that Paul is still alive. Don't you see? You're still alive, Paul. You're still alive!"

Without thinking, she ran over to him and happily threw her arms around his shoulders[3]. She felt nothing, nothing but cold air. Feeling foolish, she stepped back. He was looking hard at her, still thinking about what she had said.

"In other words," he said slowly, "you haven't killed me yet."

His words sent a chill down her back. She dropped onto her bed. "No," she said quietly, "I haven't killed you yet. That's why I had no memory of it. I haven't done it."

"But you're going to." He stared at her accusingly. "You're going to."

"No!" she cried. "No! Don't say that! I won't! I can't! I promise I won't!"

"I'm dead, trapped here," he said, "and you did it."

---

1 **past** – *Vergangenheit*
2 **to avenge sth.** – *etw. rächen*
3 **to throw one's arms around sb.'s shoulder** – *jdm. um den Hals fallen*

"No!" Melissa cried. The thought of killing Paul—of killing anyone—was too terrifying[1] to think about. "No! Please, listen! Don't you see? This is a second chance, Paul, for both of us. I won't kill you. Just stay away! If you're not here, there's no way I could kill you."

"I'm already a ghost," Paul said sadly. "It's the live Paul who has to stay away."

"Of course. Don't you see? That's why you've come back. You didn't come back to earth to kill me and avenge your death. You came back to earth to prevent[2] your death! You can do it! You can stop yourself from getting killed!"

His smile was radiant[3], mixed with the sunlight streaming into the room, a white light, so bright Melissa had to shield her eyes with her hand. When she lowered her hand, Paul was standing in front of her. It was his turn to try to hug her. He leaned down. His arms went around her shoulders. "Can you feel anything?"

"Yes," she answered. "It isn't cold. The air is warm now. I can almost feel you, Paul."

"I'm getting strong again. Thank you," he said, smiling.

"I didn't really do anything," she said. She realized, to her surprise, that she cared about what happened to him.

"Yeah, you did. You helped figure this all out. You've given me a second chance. And I'm not going to blow it[4]."

"I'll help," she said, thinking about how sweet and boyish[5] he was once you got past the tough exterior, the bitterness in his eyes. "I'll take you to him. I'll take you to the live Paul, tonight! You've got to warn him. You've got to stop him from getting killed!"

According to Melissa's theory, is Paul still alive? Why?

---

1   **terrifying –** *entsetzlich*
2   **to prevent sth. –** *etw. verhindern*
3   **radiant –** *strahlend*
4   **to blow sth. –** *etw. vermasseln*
5   **boyish –** *jungenhaft*

CHAPTER 17

Paul's house stood in a line of clapboard¹ houses in a run-down²
neighborhood west of the Old Village. A few stoops down the row, two
teenage girls in jeans and black leather jackets were having a loud argument,
ignoring³ a neighbor, who was pleading for them to shut up.

Melissa parked the car and locked it. She wondered if the car would be okay
in this neighborhood.

At first, Paul didn't recognize the house. "This isn't it."

"But you said Frankie was your neighbor, right?" Melissa insisted. "Well, I
looked up Frankie's address in the phone book. He lives at thirty-six. So
your house must be thirty-four or thirty-eight."

Paul, his face as gray as the evening light, shook his head uncertainly and
looked up at the dark, dirty windows of the houses. "Maybe," he said
finally, his voice a whisper.

Two teenage boys, wearing only jeans and T-shirts despite the coolness of
the evening, came running at full speed⁴ around the corner. Melissa had to
jump to the side to get out of their way. They laughed and kept running.

To her surprise, Paul was already halfway up the steps to number thirty-
four. "This is it," he said. "Yes. This is my house. There's my name on the
mailbox. Starett. All of a sudden, I have all these memories." He didn't seem
happy about them, only overwhelmed⁵, filled with sadness, with
apprehension⁶. "I'm going in," he said. "Come with me."

"I can't," she called up to him. "He'll see me."

He looked down at her from the top of the stoop. "You're right. Wait for
me. Wish me luck." He tried to make it sound light, but his trembling voice
revealed⁷ how worried he was.

---

1 **clapboard** – *Schindel*
2 **run-down** – *heruntergekommen*
3 **to ignore** – *jdn. nicht beachten*
4 **at full speed** – *mit voller Geschwindigkeit*
5 **overwhelmed** – *überwältigt*
6 **apprehension** – *Besorgnis, Befürchtung*
7 **to reveal** – *enthüllen*

"Good luck," Melissa said, sitting down on a cold step. She watched him walk through the front door without opening it. If he succeeds[1], if he can communicate with the live Paul, he'll go away and I'll never see him again, she thought. To her surprise, she wasn't sure how she felt about that.

The ghost Paul floated through his old living room, dark and empty. The furniture looked familiar even though a few seconds earlier he had no recollection of any of it.

Without realizing it, he cried out. It was as if he were dying all over again[2], losing everything that mattered[3] to him.

I can't go through with this, he thought. It's just too painful. He heard a noise in the back. The sound of shoes scraping against the floor. A cough. He moved away from the old couch and headed towards it. His bedroom was there, he suddenly remembered. He could picture it so clearly. The long, narrow[4] room. The bunk bed[5] against the wall. The folding chair[6] in front of the white counter that served[7] as his desk.

The door to his room was open. The light was on. He hesitated a few feet from the door. He could feel his energy level surge. He slid silently through the doorway and floated into the narrow room.

And saw—himself.

Sitting on the lower bunk, there he was. How strange to walk into a room and find yourself. How frightening.

How sad.

The ghost Paul drifted[8] closer, into the center of the narrow room. The living Paul tilted[9] a beer can up to his mouth until it was empty and then tossed it toward the waste-basket across the room.

---

1   **to succeed –** *Erfolg haben*
2   **all over again –** *noch einmal, aufs Neue*
3   **to matter to sb. –** *jdm. wichtig sein*
4   **narrow –** *schmal*
5   **bunk bed –** *Etagenbett*
6   **folding chair –** *Klappstuhl*
7   **to serve as sth. –** *als etw. dienen*
8   **to drift –** *(hier:) schweben*
9   **to tilt –** *kippen*

He was dressed identically to the ghost, his denim jacket open to reveal a yellow T-shirt underneath, his jeans faded and stained. He ran his hands back through his long, black hair and stood up.

The ghost started to call to him, then stopped. Paul had walked to the kitchen and got the phone book out. He opened it and began searching for a name, moving his finger slowly down the columns.

Then he picked up the phone, an uncertain look on his face. He dialed[1].

"Hello. Is Melissa there?"

"No. This is just a friend," Paul said, sounding disappointed. "My name? It doesn't matter." He hung up the receiver and kicked the cupboard angrily. Then, looking out the window, he started to button his jacket.

He's going out. I'd better materialize now, the ghost thought. He stepped in front of Paul.

"Don't be afraid."

Paul finished buttoning his jacket, turned, and headed out the kitchen door.

"Can you hear me?" the ghost called, following behind him.

Paul quickly walked back to his room, picked up a hairbrush from the dresser[2] top, and, tilting his head to the side, began brushing his dark hair straight back.

"Turn around!" the ghost yelled. "You've got to hear me. You've got to!"

Whistling to himself, Paul tilted his head the other way and continued to brush his hair.

Desperately, the ghost grabbed at the hairbrush. But his hand went right through it. "Please—turn around! Can't you hear me?"

The ghost concentrated his energy, tried harder to appear. But Paul just turned off the lamp and headed down the long hall, then out the front door. He floated through the front wall of the house. Paul was already down the steps and jogging toward Davis Street. Melissa was nowhere to be seen. Paul entered Aldo's, the liquor store[3] on the corner. A minute later he came out carrying a brown paper bag. Walking jauntily[4], he headed out to the

---

1 **to dial** – *wählen*
2 **dresser** – *Kommode*
3 **liquor store** – *Getränkeminimarkt, Kiosk*
4 **jauntily** – *flott, schwungvoll*

parking lot at the side of the store. "Hey, Kenny, Frankie—what are you bozos[1] doing here?"

"You got beer?" Frankie asked, grabbing at the bag.

"Not for you," Paul told him. "Beer makes you drool[2]."

"So?"

"Where's your rich girlfriend?" Kenny asked Paul.

Paul flashed him a dirty look. "Who?"

"That rich girl with all the hair."

Frankie and Kenny both burst into high-pitched laughter and slapped each other a hard high-five[3]. Frankie made another unsuccessful grab for the beer.

"I can have her anytime I want," Paul bragged[4], tapping himself on the chest. His two friends laughed again.

"Then how come she came to see me?" Frankie asked, grinning. "This morning. At the supermarket."

"So *that's* why she was at the supermarket." Paul glared. "What'd she want?"

"Give me a beer and I'll tell you," Frankie said.

"Me too," Kenny added quickly, reaching out[5].

"Tell me, or you'll be eating the cans," Paul said menacingly.

The grins faded from their faces. It was obvious that they were afraid of him. "She came to ask me about you."

"What'd she want to know?" Paul demanded.

"Hey, you guys, get moving[6]. Don't hang around here."

They looked up to see a policeman's head poking out[7] of a black-and-white cruiser. "We were just going, Officer," Paul said politely, hiding the bag containing the six-pack behind his jacket. They piled into Kenny's old Chevy Malibu, parked at the edge of the lot. The ghost Paul followed, wondering how to reach the live Paul. But he sank deeper into despair[8], feeling that he was destined to fail[9].

---

1 **bozo –** *(ugs.) Niete*
2 **to drool –** *sabbern*
3 **to slap a high-five –** *abklatschen*
4 **to brag –** *prahlen, angeben*
5 **to reach out –** *die Hand ausstrecken*
6 **to get moving –** *(ugs.) in die Gänge kommen*
7 **to poke out of sth. –** *aus etw. herausragen*
8 **despair –** *Verzweiflung*
9 **destined to fail –** *zum Scheitern verurteilt*

"Where we going?" Paul asked, seated beside his ghost in the backseat.

"We can't go anywhere. No money," Frankie said.

"Well, there are ways to get money," Paul said, grinning.

More memories came rushing back to the silent ghost at Paul's side, memories of scrambling[1] through windows, of desperate, dark searches.

"You really break into houses?" Frankie asked, turning around in the passenger seat to look at Paul.

Paul nodded, swallowing a mouthful of beer. "Sure."

"All those houses on Fear Street?" Kenny asked, impressed. "So those stories in the paper are about you?"

"I said there are ways to get money," Paul said smugly[2].

"They're calling you the Fear Street Prowler," Kenny said.

Paul's words opened up more memories for his ghost. Of course. How could he have forgotten? He–Paul–was the Fear Street Prowler. But now he had to stop Paul. He had to keep him away from Fear Street. But how? Everything went white. He was leaving them, leaving the car, drifting into the blank[3] world where he spent so much of his time. Struggling[4] to stay with his live self, the ghost faded. When he returned, it was some time later. The car was parked by the side of a road.

Where were they? The ghost could see a tilted street sign up ahead, Fear Street. He floated over the lawn as Paul made his way around the side of the rambling old house, keeping against the wall, in the shadows. He was about to break into a house.

No, thought the ghost. I've got to stop this. These break-ins[5] will lead to his – to my – death. But what can I do?

In the dark he saw a rake tilted against the house a few feet from where Paul stood. I'll swing[6] the rake, he thought. If I can frighten him, maybe he won't break into this house.

Since fading into the blank, white world, he felt stronger. Strong enough to

---

1   **to scramble through sth. –** *sich durch etw. zwängen*
2   **smugly –** *selbstgefällig*
3   **blank –** *leer*
4   **to struggle to do sth. –** *Mühe haben, etwas zu tun*
5   **break-in –** *Einbruch*
6   **to swing –** *schwingen, schwenken*

lift the rake. He drifted toward it, summoned[1] his energy, wrapped himself around the handle, and tugged – and he was moving it. Finally, he thought. Finally I can get through to Paul.

He pulled the rake away from the wall, raised it in the air, and saw that he was too late. Paul was slipping through the window into the dark house. Too late. The ghost dropped the rake, suddenly feeling powerless and defeated[2].

When the woman's screams shattered the silence[3] of the night air, he didn't move. A second scream. The sound of shattering glass. And Paul came flying out of a window, rolling as he hit the ground, on his feet in seconds, and running toward the street. The screams continued. "Help! Help me! Please, somebody–help me!"

The ghost watched Paul run to the car and pull the back door open. The old Malibu roared away, its lights off, the back door still open. Lights came on all over the house, but the ghost didn't move. He floated somewhere between this world and another, his mind in turmoil[4], feeling so light, so invisible, so helpless–so lifeless.

* * *

"Where'd you go?" the ghost asked.

Melissa cried out. "You scared me!" She had just washed her hair and had a green bath towel wrapped around her head. She wore a blue bathrobe[5] over her pajamas.

"Sorry," the ghost said softly.

"I couldn't wait for you. It was too creepy there," she said, apologizing[6] as she sat down on the edge of the bed.

"It's where I grew up," he said bitterly.

"Please don't be angry," she said.

"I spent my whole life angry," the ghost said. The darkness from outside the window seemed to seep[7] into him until he was all shadows. "Being poor can make you angry."

---

1 **to summon** – *zusammennehmen*
2 **defeated** – *geschlagen*
3 **to shatter a silence** – *die Stille zerreißen*
4 **turmoil** – *Aufruhr*
5 **bathrobe** – *Bademantel*
6 **to apologize** – *sich entschuldigen*
7 **to seep** – *sickern*

"Are you going to start putting me down[1] again for being rich?" she asked wearily.

"No." The shadows darkened. His voice grew even softer, more distant. "I know you're different. But what difference does it make?" he moaned.

"What happened after I left? Could he see you?"

"No," the ghost explained. "There was no way. I can't change anything. I'm going to be killed–again."

"No! I won't kill him! I won't kill you!" Melissa cried.

"You won't be able to help it," Paul said bitterly.

"Then I'll go talk to him," Melissa said impulsively[2], playing with the silver pendant around her neck. "I'll go tell him to stay away from Fear Street. I'm not invisible."

"Why should he listen to you?"

"I'll reason with him."

"Don't be stupid."

Melissa looked hurt. "I'm not being stupid. I'm trying to help. You couldn't get through to him. So who else is there to try? Only me. Think I want to go see him? No way."

"You're doing this for me?" The ghost sounded moved[3].

Melissa flushed[4]. "Well, yes. But I'm also doing it for me. I'm frightened that you may be right. I don't want to kill anyone. I don't want your story to come true. If there's anything I can do to stop it from happening, I will."

The ghost started to fade. "Forget it. We can't change anything," he said sadly and then vanished completely.

How does the ghost try to stop Paul breaking into the house when he realises he cannot talk to him?

---

1 **to put sb. down** – *jdn. herunterputzen*
2 **impulsive** – *impulsiv, spontan*
3 **moved** – *bewegt, gerührt*
4 **to flush** – *erröten, rot werden*

CHAPTER 18

It was the next night. Melissa was preparing to drive to Paul's. She tried to brush her hair, which was sticking up[1] on both sides like two airplane wings. "No really, Buddy, I can't," she said, trying not to sound annoyed.

Why did Buddy have to sound so concerned about her every time they spoke? They couldn't have a normal conversation anymore. All he did was worry about her and ask questions to find out if she had stopped seeing ghosts.

"Maybe we can go out tomorrow night," she said. "Call me at Delia's. I'll be staying there while my parents are in Las Vegas. I really have to go now." And she hung up.

Maybe I *am* crazy, she thought. Driving off past the Old Village to that horrible neighborhood to see that creep. He's just going to tease me and say that I'm coming on to him again, and it's going to be very unpleasant. And if he doesn't listen to me, is it possible that I really am going to kill him? No. No way. No way I'm going to kill *anyone*, not Paul, not anyone. No matter how many times she assured[2] herself, there was still a lingering[3] doubt in her mind. And the only way to get rid of that doubt was to talk to Paul.

Melissa climbed the steps up to Paul's front door. It was a cool night, almost cold, a preview[4] of autumn nights to come. She looked for a doorbell, but not finding one knocked loudly, louder than she had intended. She glanced nervously down the block, pulling down the sleeves of the Shadyside High sweatshirt she was wearing.

She knocked again. The house was dark. He isn't home, she thought, both disappointed and relieved. What would I say to him anyway? She had tried to rehearse[5] in the car, but hadn't come up with anything that didn't sound totally stupid. With a loud sigh, she turned and walked down the stairs. She

---

1   **to stick up –** *abstehen*
2   **to assure oneself –** *(hier:) sich zusichern*
3   **lingering –** *verbleibend*
4   **preview –** *Vorschau*
5   **to rehearse –** *vorbereiten, proben*

had started to unlock[1] her car when she heard laughter at the end of the block.

At first she ignored it. She started to slide behind the wheel when she heard it again. She thought she recognized Paul's laugh and climbed back out of the car. It was a short walk to the corner. Why not see if it's him?

Walking quickly, she came to a small liquor store on the corner, a neon sign in the window reading Aldo's. Illuminated[2] by a low street lamp, three boys were leaning against a red Malibu in the parking lot, laughing and drinking. They turned immediately when Melissa came into view, and stopped laughing. The boy in the middle, sitting on the front bumper[3], was Paul. He stood up and a smile crossed his face. It was too late to go back to the car.

"Look who's here!" one of the other boys shouted. Melissa recognized Frankie, the boy from the supermarket. She didn't know the third boy.

"You following me?" Paul called to her, straightening his dark hair. The other two boys laughed as he stood up and swayed[4] as he walked toward Melissa. She realized he must have had a lot to drink already.

"I–I wanted to talk to you," she said, staying on the sidewalk near the street lamp, not going any closer.

"She wants you, Paul," the two boys laughed, banging their open hands on the car. Paul ignored them and kept walking slowly, unsteadily toward Melissa. She stood her ground[5], determined to say what she had to say. He looked so much like his ghost, but without the tenderness in his eyes, without the boyishness.

"Hey," he said, stopping a few inches in front of her. "You didn't answer my question. You following me?"

"Paul, if you'd just let me–"

"How'd you know my name? How'd you know where I was? What do you want anyway?" He smiled, more a smirk[6] than a smile. "You don't have to answer me. You want to go somewhere quiet and have a talk?"

---

1 **to unlock** – *aufmachen*
2 **illuminated** – *beleuchtet*
3 **bumper** – *Stoßstange*
4 **to sway** – *schwanken*
5 **to stand one's ground** – *nicht von der Stelle weichen*
6 **smirk** – *spöttisches Grinsen*

He grabbed her wrist. The two boys back in the parking lot cheered. He glanced back at them, tightening his grip on her wrist. "Let's lose those guys," he said, pulling her.

"No. Let go."

He didn't let go. "Hey, you came to see me, right?"

"Yes. I have something very important to– Stop. You're hurting me, Paul."

"No pain, no gain," he muttered and laughed. Still holding her wrist, he pulled her close to him. "You want to talk? We'll talk, Melissa. Just the two of us." He pulled her away from the parking lot, away from the streetlight, into the dark. She pulled back, staring into his face, and froze with fear. He looked so angry, so out of control.

> How does Melissa find Paul outside the liquor store)?

CHAPTER 19

TR. 19

"I found your house. On Fear Street."

"That's what I want to talk to you about," Melissa said.

"You found *my* house, right?" He was twisting[1] her arm. "So I found yours. That's fair, don't you think?"

Melissa gave a hard tug and pulled free. They were in front of her car now. She began to feel a little safer.

"I want you to leave me alone," she said.

He laughed. "That's why you came to see me?" He put his hands in his pockets, then took them out.

"Please, don't laugh at me. I'm very serious. Leave me alone. Stay away from my house. It's very important."

Paul leaned toward her. "I don't get it."

---

1 **to twist –** *verdrehen*

"I really can't explain," she said. "I'm just warning you—"

"You're warning me?" he exploded. "You come to my neighborhood? You follow me? You're warning me?"

"You don't understand. It's for your own good. Just stay away from Fear Street."

She knew all along that she was bound[1] to sound stupid.

I just want to be away from here, she thought.

"Don't worry. I'll wipe my feet before I come to your street," Paul said bitterly, staring past her. His face turned angry. He called her an ugly name, then turned and started back toward the parking lot.

"Please listen to me," she called after him, feeling like a fool. But what could she have said? That his ghost had come to her? For sure. That would really make the right impression. He's so tanked up[2] on beer, he probably won't even remember that I was here, she thought.

Suddenly feeling very tired, she climbed into the car and headed for home. Paul's ghost warned me that I wouldn't get through to him, she thought. He was right.

The next evening Delia called just before dinner. "Oh, hi, Delia," Melissa said. "I'll be over right after dinner. I'm all packed for the weekend. I have so much to tell you—"

"There's a slight hitch[3]," Delia interrupted. "I'm still at my cousin's. I won't be back in Shadyside till tomorrow."

"You mean—" Melissa couldn't hide her disappointment.

"Think you could stay home tonight and come tomorrow?" Delia asked. "I'm really sorry."

"No problem," Melissa said. "But I don't think I'll tell my parents. They'll only worry." Besides, she thought, I won't be alone. Paul is here.

"I'm really worried about you," Mrs. Dryden said as she and Mr. Dryden were about to leave for the airport.

---

1 **to be bound to do sth.** – *zwangsläufig etw. machen*
2 **tanked up** – *(ugs.) voll*
3 **slight hitch** – *kleiner Haken*

"Mother, I'll be fine. Really." Melissa sat down at the bottom of the stairs and watched her father struggle to close the suitcase.

"Well, what with this Fear Street Prowler still around–"

"Do you have to bring that up?" Mr. Dryden snapped. "Melissa isn't even staying here. She'll be with Delia."

"I just said I was worried. There was a story in the paper yesterday about him. He broke into a house just down the block. And the woman was home and surprised him."

"I really don't see the point of discussing the Fear Street Prowler now," Mr. Dryden told his wife. He turned to Melissa. "You *will* remember to lock both doors, right?"

"Right," Melissa said, rolling her eyes.

"When are you going to Delia's? Are you packed?" her mother asked.

"Yes, I'm packed." That was the truth. "I'm going over there soon after you leave." That wasn't quite the truth.

"Well, we'll call you tomorrow," Mrs. Dryden said.

"Mother, I'm not ten years old, you know. I really can manage."

Finally they drove off, after giving Melissa a few more warnings, reminding her she could call her aunt Kate if she had any problems, and telling her again where they had written down the phone number of the hotel in Las Vegas.

Melissa watched them back down the drive. Then she closed the front door and locked it.

All alone now. Even Marta had left for a few days to see her brother in Cincinnati. All alone. Except for a ghost.

She walked into the den, searched through the stack of CDs, and put one on the player. Music flooded the room. Loud, pounding dance music. She danced across the floor by herself for a few seconds. She felt like dancing. Where was Buddy? They could go back to Red Heat and dance till they dropped[1]. Then she wouldn't feel so nervous. Red Heat made her think of Paul and his friends out in the parking lot. The loud music was making her nervous. She danced over to the CD player and shut it off.

---

[1] **till they dropped –** *(ugs.) bis sie nicht mehr konnten*

What should she do? She paced back and forth in the den. But that was only making her feel more nervous. This is crazy, she thought. I'm an intelligent person. I should be able to entertain myself for one evening without going nuts. She got a Coke from the refrigerator in the kitchen, then went up to her room to read in bed. She started to get undressed. Then stopped.

"Hey, Paul–are you here?"

There was no reply. She walked around the room, checking to see if there was a spot of cold air, a sign that the ghost was there.

"Paul?"

Where was he? Wasn't he at all interested in what had happened the night before? And where did the ghost go when he wasn't there? Did he just fade into nothingness? Or was he always around, always watching her? Did he watch her undress? The idea was sort of exciting.

Maybe he's here, watching me now. "Paul?"

She decided to lock the window. Outside, she saw that it was a clear night, hot and still. Nothing moved. Not even a tree leaf. It was so still, it looked unreal. Feeling strange, she took a long sip of the Coke. "I'll just go to sleep," she said aloud. She looked at the clock. It was eleven-thirty. Early, but she could probably fall asleep.

She got changed into an old pajama shirt and slid under the covers. The bed felt warm, too warm. She kicked the covers down to the foot of the bed and turned off the lamp.

She closed her eyes, tried to relax. But it was too hot. With a loud sigh, she climbed out of bed, walked over to the window, unlocked it, and pulled it up halfway. There was no breeze at all and back in bed, the sheets were damp[1] from her sweat.

I can't sleep in here, she decided. She got up and, without turning on a light, padded[2] across the carpeted hall to her parents' air-conditioned[3] room. Yawning loudly, she climbed under the soft, cool sheet. The bed felt big and safe. The room was dark and fragrant from her mother's perfume. She felt snug[4], like a little girl. She drifted off into a dreamless sleep.

---

1 **damp** – *feucht*
2 **to pad** – *trotten*
3 **air-conditioned** – *klimatisiert*
4 **snug** – *gemütlich*

The noise woke her up. The digital clock on her father's bed table said 12:13. She sat up, confused at first, uncertain of where she was. The noise again. A scrabbling outside, against the side of the house. Something moved behind the window curtains. Melissa knew immediately what was happening. Someone was trying to open her parents' bedroom window.

Why does Natalie end up alone at home while her parents are in Las Vegas?

CHAPTER 20

The Fear Street Prowler!
Was this really happening?
She heard the scrabbling sounds again, and a loud noise that she recognized as a ladder[1] being banged against the clapboards. It all seemed to be happening in slow motion[2]. She looked at the clock: still 12:13. Time wasn't moving at all!
She suddenly felt as if her heart had stopped too. Frozen at 12:13. I've stopped breathing, she thought. I can't breathe. I can't move. She forced herself to stand up. She took a deep breath. Then another.
"Paul?" she called to the ghost in a quavering voice. "Paul? Help me!"
No reply. With a trembling hand, she reached over and turned on the lamp on the bed table. Maybe that would discourage him. Maybe the light would make him go away. She stood there, frozen by the bed, watching the window. Go away, go away, go away.
She saw an arm reach up from outside the window and push the window open. Then she saw the long, black hair. Then the denim jacket.

---

1   **ladder –** *Leiter*
2   **slow motion –** *Zeitlupe*

He stepped easily into the room, the curtains billowing[1] behind him.

"Paul!"

He brushed off his jeans and scowled at her.

Was it the ghost? Or was it the live Paul?

"I told you," he said, staring into her eyes. "I told you I knew where you lived."

It was the live Paul.

"Get out of here, Paul," Melissa said. She hadn't moved from beside the bed. "Get out of my house!"

She realized she was only slightly relieved that it was Paul and not the Fear Street Prowler. Paul looked dangerous. And so cold, Melissa thought. Cold and calm, not the least bit nervous about breaking into my house.

He stepped to the center of the room. His dark hair fell over his forehead.

"I told you I knew," he repeated.

"Please, Paul—"

"I'm not good enough for you, huh?"

"Let's not talk about it now, okay?" She backed away from him until she was against the wall. "You've been drinking and—and I just want you to go."

"But I've come to show you how good I am." His mouth formed an ugly smile, a cold, menacing smile.

"Paul, I'll call the police."

He snickered[2]. "I'm too fast for the police."

"Go home, Paul, and I won't tell anyone you did this."

I'm all alone here, she thought suddenly. I'm all alone in this house with him. She had stood up to him—till now. She could feel the bravery [3]wearing off and feel terror taking over. He could do anything, she thought, watching him come toward her.

She remembered her vow to the ghost: "I would never kill you. Never. Never. Never." But watching this smirking, cold-eyed Paul approach, the words seemed empty, false.

What if he tried to kill *her*? Would she fight back? Would she defend herself? No. No. No. This can't be happening. I can't kill him.

---

1 **to billow –** *sich blähen*
2 **to snicker –** *kichern*
3 **bravery –** *Mut*

But what if…

"Come on, Melissa. No more teasing. No more games. Tonight's the night."

"No. Just turn around and go back out the window."

"But I'm good enough for you, Melissa. You'll see. I'm real good." He spoke quietly, but his eyes revealed excitement, every word sounded like a threat. Suddenly a picture flashed into Melissa's mind. The pistol. The little silver pistol.

It was right there in front of her, just a few feet away in her father's night table. Waiting for her. Waiting to protect her from Paul. No. No. No way. She wouldn't shoot it, of course. She would only use it to frighten him away[1]. And she was so totally alone. Did she really have a choice?

Was she about to make the ghost's prediction come true?

I don't care, she thought, staring at Paul, reading the hatred in his eyes. I have to protect myself.

I don't care. I don't care. I don't care.

No. No. I can't.

She stood frozen against the wall, at war with herself, watching him approach. Then, without consciously[2] making the decision, she dived forward[3] and pulled open the drawer. There it was. Waiting. Waiting for her. The small pistol seemed to shine in the lamplight. She hesitated for only a second. Then she grabbed it. It felt cool in the palm of her hand[4].

Paul grinned at her from across the bed. She raised the pistol, and his grin slowly faded.

"Get out, Paul," she cried, her voice trembling. She held the little pistol with both hands to keep it steady. "Get out right now. I mean it."

"Whoa, babe[5]." He raised his hands, as if in surrender[6].

"Out. Get out." She took a cautious step toward him, pointing the pistol at him[7], studying his face. He stared into her eyes and slowly lowered his hands. He seemed to be thinking it over, deciding what to do.

---

1   **to frighten sb. away –** *jdn. vertreiben*
2   **conscious –** *bewusst*
3   **to dive forward –** *sich vorwärtsstürzen*
4   **palm of one's hand –** *Handinnenfläche*
5   **babe –** *(ugs.) Süße, Schatz*
6   **surrender –** *Kapitulation*
7   **to point sth. at sb. –** *etw. auf jdn. richten*

"Go now and I won't tell anyone you did this," Melissa repeated. She gestured[1] with the gun toward the door.

But he didn't leave the room. Instead he walked up to the bed, grabbed the bedspread and tugged it off the bed. He let it drop to the floor and ran his hand[2] over the smooth, pale blue sheets.

"Paul, what do you think you're doing?"

He smiled at her, his hand still on the sheet. "Nice bed."

"I'm warning you—"

"Why don't you and me…" He patted the bed.

She uttered a low cry and ran to the door. She didn't have a plan. She just knew she had to get out. But he moved quickly and blocked the doorway. Melissa couldn't stop herself. She ran right into him.

"You're not going anywhere," he said, grabbing her by the shoulders and shoving her back. She stumbled, but caught her balance[3] against the foot of the bed.

She gestured with the pistol. "Out. Get out." Her voice revealed how terrified she was.

He took a few slow, casual[4] steps toward her. "Go ahead," he said, an odd smile on his face.

"What?"

"Go ahead. Use the gun. Shoot me."

Melissa kept it pointed at his chest. "Think I won't?"

He took a step toward her, then another.

"Paul—no."

He came closer, and closer. He was laughing at her now, challenging[5] her, daring[6] her to shoot him.

"Come on, girl. Shoot me. Use the gun."

"No. Stop right there. I mean it, Paul."

But he kept coming, one step at a time.

---

1   **to gesture –** *deuten*
2   **to run one's hand over sth –** *mit der Hand über etw. fahren*
3   **to catch one's balance –** *das Gleichgewicht wiederfinden*
4   **casual –** *beiläufig*
5   **to challenge sb. –** *jdn. herausfordern*
6   **to dare sb. to do sth. –** *jdn. dazu herausfordern, etw. zu tun*

Her hand tensed[1]. The gun was pointed at his chest, just inches away from him.

All she had to do was pull the trigger[2].

But she knew she couldn't do it. No way. She couldn't pull the trigger. She would never be able to pull the trigger.

She started to lower the gun.

"No. I can't use it."

"Then *I'll* use it!" Paul cried, grabbing at the pistol. She tried to pull her hand away, but was too slow. His hand missed the gun and slapped[3] against hers.

The pistol dropped to the carpet.

They both stared down at it for a long second.

Then they both dived to the floor, scrambling frantically to reach it first.

What does Melissa take from her father's bedside drawer?

CHAPTER 21

TR. 21

"Ow!"

Melissa's elbow hit the floor hard as she dived. The pain shot up her arm as she reached for the pistol.

I've got it! she thought.

But with an angry groan, Paul shoved her away. The gun fell out of her hand, and he picked it up. Breathing hard, his face red, he stood above her, waving the pistol in front of him. "You rich snob! You're dead now!"

He kicked at her, but Melissa rolled away and climbed quickly to her feet. They stared at each other, breathing noisily.

---

1   **to tense –** *sich anspannen*
2   **to pull the trigger –** *abdrücken*
3   **to slap –** *klatschen*

"What good is all your money now?" he cried.

Melissa took a step back, eyeing the door. "Put down the gun, Paul. You're not going to use it either."

His eyes flared. "Want to bet?" He called her a stream of names[1].

He could do it. He could shoot me.

The bedroom door seemed so far away. And he was standing between her and the door. She held up her hands as if to say, Okay, I give up.

His finger tightened on the trigger.

He's going to shoot me, Melissa thought. I'm going to die now.

She closed her eyes.

When she opened them, the ghost was standing next to Paul. She blinked, thinking she was seeing double[2] at first. Flickering[3] in and out of view, the ghost stared first at her, then at Paul. "No! I can't let this happen!" the ghost cried.

Paul didn't react. Melissa realized he couldn't see the ghost. He kept the pistol aimed[4] at her chest.

"I can't let him do this to you!" the ghost cried. Melissa tried to scream, but no sound came out. The ghost lunged forward and reached for the pistol in Paul's hand. Melissa expected his hand to sail right through the pistol. But it didn't.

The live Paul cried out in surprise as the gun flew from his hand. With one quick motion[5], the ghost pulled the pistol away and tossed it toward Melissa. "Hey, what the—" Paul cried.

The gun flew across the room. Melissa had to jump up to catch it. As her hands wrapped[6] around it, the gun went off.

"No!" Her scream was as loud as the explosion of sound between her hands. Paul groaned loudly and grabbed his chest. A dark red circle formed on the front of the denim jacket. "Oh, no," he groaned. "Not me…"

He dropped to his knees. Blood trickled[7] down onto the white carpet. Holding his chest, he fell face forward onto the rug. He didn't move.

---

1   **steam of names –** *Aneinanderreihung von Beleidigungen*
2   **to see double –** *doppelt sehen*
3   **to flicker –** *flackern*
4   **aimed –** *gerichtet*
5   **with one motion –** *mit einer einzigen Bewegung*
6   **to wrap around sth. –** *sich um etw. wickeln*
7   **to trickle –** *tropfen*

"Paul—" Melissa let the gun fall to the floor. She ran to him, bent down over him, turned him over. He was dead.

How does Paul's ghost help to kill Paul?

CHAPTER 22

Melissa stepped back from the body. She looked down and saw that her bare[1] feet were stained with blood. The ghost was right beside her, staring down at Paul's body.

"So that's how it happened," he said, his voice a soft, stunned[2] whisper.

"But why? Why did you sacrifice[3] yourself?"

He didn't answer.

"Why did you knock the gun away, Paul? Why did you *let* me kill you?" He stood so close to her, yet the air wasn't cold. "You knew I would kill Paul if you took the gun from him."

"Yes, I knew what would happen," he said, turning to look into her eyes.

"But I couldn't let him kill you. I—I care about you too much."

"I care about you too," Melissa cried.

The ghost pulled her close and wrapped his arms around her. He pulled her face up to his and they kissed.

"I can feel you, Paul!" Melissa cried. "I can feel you now." She reached for him, but he floated away from her, a sad smile on his face.

"I–I'm going, Melissa. I think I can rest[4] now. I've been so unhappy. Caught between two worlds. Not knowing why. Not knowing what happened to me. Thank God it's over."

"But, Paul—"

---

1   **bare –** *nackt*
2   **stunned –** *fassungslos*
3   **to sacrifice oneself –** *sich aufopfern*
4   **to rest –** *ruhen*

"I won't forget you. I won't ever forget you. Don't feel guilty[1] for killing me. Don't ever feel guilty. You were the only one who ever cared about me. The only one ..." The words faded as he did.

He was a shadow, then the outline of a shadow. And then he was gone. She stood staring at the spot where he had stood. She could still feel his arms around her, still feel the warmth[2] of his lips.

But she knew he was gone forever.

It took her a long time to realize that someone was pounding on the front door. Who could it be this late?

She stepped around Paul's body and ran to the bedroom window. "Buddy!"

He backed up to the edge of the porch and looked up.

"Buddy, what are you doing here? How did you–"

"Lissa, are you okay?" he shouted up to her. "I went over to Delia's, but you weren't there. I got worried, so I came here. When I got out of my car, I heard a loud noise–like a gunshot[3]. I was so worried–"

"I-I'm okay," she called down. "I'm so glad to see you."

She ran down the stairs and pulled open the front door. "I'm so glad you're here," she repeated. "I need help."

She led[4] him up to her parents' bedroom. He stopped short when he saw the body on the carpet. He grabbed her arm, his face filled with confusion.

"Lissa, is that your ghost?"

"No," she said. "That's not him. The ghost is gone, Buddy. Gone for good. That's just some prowler."

"I'm so glad you're okay," he said, putting his arm around her. "Thank God it's over."

That's just what Paul said, Melissa thought. She leaned against Buddy as they walked downstairs to call the police.

Why did Paul's ghost help to kill Paul?

---

1   **to feel guilty** – *sich schuldig fühlen*
2   **warmth** – *Wärme*
3   **gunshot** – *Schuss*
4   **to lead sb. to sth.** – *jdn. zu etw. führen*

NÜTZLICHE WÖRTER UND WENDUNGEN ZUM THEMA "HORROR"

accident – Unfall
to be afraid – Angst haben
basement – Keller
to choke – würgen
chilling – schaurig
  It sends a chill down my spine. –
  Mir läuft dabei ein Schauer über den
  Rücken.
coffin – Sarg
corpse – Leiche
to creep – kriechen
creepy – gruselig, unheimlich
  It creeps me out! – Mir gruselts!
crooked – krumm
dread – Angst, Grauen
escape – entkommen
fear – Furcht, Angst
frightening – beängstigend
funeral – Beerdigung
ghastly – grausig, schrecklich
ghost – Geist, Gespenst
ghostly – gespenstisch
grave – Grab
graveyard – Friedhof

grim – düster, betrüblich
gun – Schusswaffe
to haunt – heimsuchen, herumgeistern
horrifying – entsetzlich
to howl – heulen
to kill – töten, umbringen
killer – Totschläger
knife – Messer
murder – Mord
to murder – ermorden
murderer – Mörder
scary – erschreckend, gruselig
  Are you scared? – Hast du Angst?
to scream – schreien
shadow – Schatten
shady – schattig, dubios
to shiver – schauern, frösteln
spell – Bann
spook – Spuk
spooky – gespenstisch
terrifying – erschreckend
to tremble – zittern
weapon – Waffe

AMERIKANISCHE UND ENGLISCHE BEGRIFFE IM ÜBERBLICK

Im Text sind einige Wörter hinterlegt. Das sind Begriffe, die so eher nur im amerikanischen Sprachraum verwendet werden. In Großbritannien benutzt man in manchen Fällen ein ganz anderes Wort. Hier siehst du, wie unterschiedlich sich Amerikaner und Briten ausdrücken würden

American English	Deutsche Übersetzung	British English
to be busted	Riesenärger bekommen	to be in big trouble
before school let out	bevor die Ferien anfingen	before school broke up
bozo	Niete	looser
buddies	Kumpel (Pl.)	mates
chips	Kartoffelchips	crips
closet	Schrank	wardrobe
cruiser	Streifenwagen	patrol car
to cut	(hier:) ausschalten	to turn off
den	Hobbyraum	hobby room
dresser	Kommode	chest of drawers
dude	Typ	bloke
gross	eklig	horrible
hood	Motorhaube	bonnet
jean cutoffs	abgeschnittene Jeans	cut-off jeans
liquor store	Kiosk, Getränkeminimarkt	off-licence
to make out	rummachen, rumknutschen	to smootch
nighttable	Nachttisch	bedside table
on tiptoe	auf Zehenspitzen	on tiptoes
pajamas	Pyjama	pyjamas
parking lot	Parkplatz	car park
shoulder	Randstreifen	verge
soda	Softgetränk	drink
to start out	herausgehen	to head out
truck	Lastwagen	transporter
vacation	Ferien, Urlaub	holiday
VCR	Videorekorder	video player
waste-basket	Abfalleimer	dustbin

ENGLISCH-DEUTSCHE WORTLISTE

	..., I'll bet	..., nicht wahr?
	accusing	anklagend, beschuldigend
	aimed	gerichtet
	air-conditioned	klimatisiert
	aisle	Gang
	alert	wachsam
	all over again	noch einmal, aufs Neue
to	annoy sb.	jdn. aufregen, stören
	apologetic	entschuldigend, unterwürfig
to	apologize	sich entschuldigen
	apprehension	Besorgnis, Befürchtung
	Are you kidding?	(ugs.) Machst du Witze?
to	argue	sich streiten
	argument	Streit
	as far as she was concerned	was sie betraf
	as if reading her mind	als ob er in ihre Gedanken lesen könnte
to	ask sb. out for dinner	jdn. auf ein Abendessen einladen
to	assure oneself	(hier:) sich zusichern
	at full speed	mit voller Geschwindigkeit
to	avenge sth.	etw. rächen
	babe	(ugs.) Süße, Schatz
to	back a car	rückwärts fahren
	back and forth	rauf und runter
to	back down	zurückweichen
to	bag groceries	Einkäufe eintüten
	bar	Theke
to	barbecue	grillen
	bare	nackt
	bathrobe	Bademantel
to	be bound to do sth.	zwangsläufig etw. machen
to	be buddies	befreundet sein
to	be busted	Riesenärger bekommen

to	be embarrassed by sth.	etw. peinlich finden
to	be nuts	ugs: einen Knall haben
to	be on the safe side	(ugs.) um auf Nummer sicher zu gehen
to	be scared silly	Todesängste ausstehen
	before school let out	vor den Ferien
to	billow	sich blähen
	bitterness	Verbitterung, Groll
	bizarre sense of humor	merkwürdiger Humor
	blank	leer
	blaring siren	Martinshorn
to	blast music	Musik rausdröhnen
to	blow sth.	etw. vermasseln
to	blush	erröten, rot werden
	board	Brett
	boarding pass	Bordkarte
to	boom	posaunen
to	borrow	leihen
	boyish	jungenhaft
	bozo	(ugs.) Niete
to	brag	prahlen, angeben
	branch	Ast
	bravery	Mut
	breakdown	Zusammenbruch
	break-in	Einbruch
	breeze	Brise
	breezy	windig
	brief glimpse	flüchtiger Blick
	bright	hell
to	bubble	Blasen werfen
	buddy	Kumpel
	bulky frame	(hier:) kräftiger Körper
	bumper	Stoßstange
	bunk bed	Etagenbett
	burglar	Einbrecher

to	burst in	*hereinplatzen*
	can	*Dose*
to	care about sb.	*sich aus jdm. etw. machen*
to	care about sth.	*sich für etw. interessieren*
	casual	*beiläufig*
to	catch one's balance	*das Gleichgewicht wiederfinden*
to	catch up	*aufholen*
	caught	*gefangen*
to	challenge sb.	*jdn. herausfordern*
to	chase after sb.	*jdm. hinterherrennen*
	checkout line	*Schlange an der Kasse*
	cheered up	*aufgemuntert*
	Chill out!	*(ugs.) Beruhige dich!*
to	chill sb.	*jdm. einen Schauer über den Rücken laufen lassen*
	choked	*erstickt*
to	circle around sb.	*um jdn. kreisen*
	clapboard	*Schindel*
	clashing colors	*Farben, die sich beißen*
to	close in on sb.	*sich auf jdn. zubewegen*
	clue	*Hinweis*
to	come onto sb.	*jdn. anmachen*
	compliment	*Kompliment*
	concern	*Besorgnis*
to	confide in sb.	*sich jdm. anvertrauen*
	confused	*verwirrt*
	conscious	*bewusst*
	convention	*Messe, Tagung*
to	convince sb.	*jdn. überzeugen*
	Cough it up!	*Spuck's aus!*
	counter	*Theke*
	couple	*Pärchen*
	court case	*Gerichtsverfahren*
to	crack up	*(ugs.) durchdrehen*

to creep	*kriechen*
creepy	*unheimlich*
to croak	*krächzen*
to cross one's arms	*die Arme verschränken*
to cross one's legs	*die Beine übereinanderschlagen*
crowded	*voll (mit Menschen)*
cruel	*böse*
curb	*Bordsteinkante*
curious	*neugierig*
damp	*feucht*
to dare sb. to do sth.	*jdn. dazu herausfordern etw. zu tun*
defeated	*geschlagen*
degrees	*Grad (hier: Grad Fahrenheit (US-ameri-kanische Temperatureinheit)*
to demonstrate	*zeigen*
den	*Hobbyraum*
to dent	*verbeulen*
dented	*verbeult*
despair	*Verzweiflung*
desperation	*Verzweiflung*
destined to fail	*zum Scheitern verurteilt*
determined	*entschlossen*
to dial	*wählen*
to dim	*dunkler werden, verlöschen*
to direct sb.	*(hier:) jdn. lotsen*
to disappear into thin air	*sich in Luft auflösen*
disappointed	*enttäuscht*
distinct	*verschieden, eindeutig*
to disturb	*stören*
to dive forward	*sich vorwärtsstürzen*
diving	*Tauchen*
dizzy	*schwindelig*
to doubt sb.	*jdm. misstrauen*
doubtful	*skeptisch*

	dresser	Kommode
to	drift	(hier:) schweben
	drive	Auffahrt
	driver's license	Führerschein
to	drool	sabbern
to	drop sb. off	jdn. zu Hause absetzen
to	duck	sich ducken
	dude	Typ
	effort	Anstrengung
	embarrassed	verlegen
	emergency call	Notruf
	emotionless	emotionslos
to	engulf	umfassen
to	escape	fliehen, entkommen
	exhausted	erschöpft
to	fade	(hier:) verblassen
to	fall silent	still werden
	false alarm	Fehlalarm
	features	Gesichtszüge
to	feel guilty	sich schuldig fühlen
	fierce	heftig, scharf, wild
to	figure sth. out	etw. herauskriegen
	filthy	dreckig
to	flare	funkeln
to	flicker	flackern
to	float	schweben
	floorboard	Diele
to	flush	erröten, rot werden
	folding chair	Klappstuhl
to	fool around	rumalbern
to	fool oneself into thinking that ...	sich vormachen, dass ...
	foolish	albern
	for your benefit	deinetwegen
	force	Gewalt, Kraft

to	force oneself to do sth.	sich dazu zwingen etw. zu tun
	forehand swing	Vorhandschlag
	forehead	Stirn
	forgiving	verzeihend
	foxy	sexy
	frame	Rahmen
	frantically	hektisch, panisch
to	frighten sb. away	jdn. vertreiben
	full moon	Vollmond
	furious	wütend
to	gasp	keuchen, nach Luft schnappen
to	gather one's strength	seine Kräfte zusammennehmen
	gentle	zart, sachte
to	gesture	deuten
to	get a break	es leicht haben
to	get moving	(ugs.) in die Gänge kommen
to	get rid of sb.	jdn. loswerden
	ghost	Geist
to	give sb. a hard time	jdm. zusetzen
to	give up	aufgeben
to	glance at sth.	einen Blick auf etw. werfen
	glare	grelles Licht
to	glare at sb.	jdn. wütend anfunkeln
	gleeful	fröhlich
to	go bananas	verrückt werden
	good taste	guter Geschmack
	gravel	Kies, Schotter
	greasy	fettig, schmierig
	grim	düster, betrüblich
to	grin	grinsen
to	grip	packen
	grip	Griff
to	groan	ächzen
	gross	eklig

	gunshot	Schuss
to	hallucinate	halluzinieren, Wahnvorstellungen haben
to	handle great	(bei Autos) sich hervorragend fahren lassen
	handsome	gutaussehend
	hasty	hastig
to	haunt	heimsuchen
to	have company	Besuch haben
to	have insurance	versichert sein
to	have the hots for sb.	in jdn. verknallt
to	head	sich auf den Weg machen
	heated	hitzig, erregt
	hesitant	zögerlich
to	hesitate	zögern
to	hide	verstecken
	high cheekbones	hohe Wangenknochen
	His hands coiled into fists.	Er ballte die Hämde zu Fäusten
	hood	(hier:) Motorhaube
to	hoot and howl	vor Lachen heulen
to	hover	schweben
	hurt	(hier:) beleidigt
	hurt	beleidigt
	I don't go along with some things.	In manchen Dingen bin ich nicht der gleichen Meinung.
	I would never treat you like that.	So würde
	I'll bet ...	(ugs.) Wetten, dass ...
to	ignore	jdn. nicht beachten
to	ignore sth.	etw. ausblenden
	illuminated	beleuchtet
to	imagine	(hier:) sich vorstellen
	impatient	ungeduldig
	impulsive	impulsiv, spontan
	in a powerful spell	unter einem mächtigen Bann
	in keeping with	passend zu

	inch	*Zoll (US-amerikanische/britische Maßeinheit)*
to	inch towards sth.	*sich etw. in kleinen Schritten nähern*
	inhuman	*übermenschlich*
to	insist	*beharren*
to	interrupt	*unterbrechen*
-	invisible	*unsichtbar*
to	invite sb. in	*jdn. hereinbitten*
	jagged	*kantig*
	jauntily	*flott, schwungvoll*
	jealous	*eifersüchtig*
	jean cutoffs	*abgeschnittene Jeans*
to	jerk	*ruckeln*
to	keep one's distance	*einen Abstand einhalten*
to	keep sth. to oneself	*etw. für sich behalten*
	kitchen counter	*Küchenarbeitsplatte*
	ladder	*Leiter*
	lane	*Spur*
	lawn	*Rasen*
to	lead sb. to sth.	*jdn. zu etw. führen*
	librarian	*Bibliothekar*
to	linger	*anhalten*
	lingering	*verbleibend*
	liquor store	*Getränkeminimarkt, Kiosk*
	loaded	*geladen*
to	lock	*abschließen*
	lonely	*einsam*
to	look past sb.	*an jdm. vorbeischauen*
to	loosen one's tie	*sich die Krawatte lockern*
to	loosen up	*lockerer werden*
to	lose one's balance	*das Gleichgewicht verlieren*
to	lunge at sb.	*sich auf jdn. stürzen*
to	make out	*rummachen*
to	make sense of sth.	*etw. zusammenreimen*

to	manage to do sth.	*etw. hinbekommen*
	mansion	*Anwesen*
to	materialize	*erscheinen*
to	matter to sb.	*jdm. wichtig sein*
	mean	*gemein*
to	mess up	*vergeigen*
	microfilm	*Mikrofilm*
to	mimic	*jdn. nachäffen*
	mindless	*(hier:) geistesabwesend*
to	motion	*bedeuten*
	moved	*bewegt, gerührt*
to	mutter	*murmeln*
	my old neighborhood	*mein altes Viertel*
	mysterious	*rätselhaft*
	narrow	*schmal*
	narrow shoulders	*schmale Schultern*
	neighborhood	*Viertel*
	obituary	*Nachruf, Todesanzeige*
	obvious	*offenkundig*
	on tiptoe	*auf Zehenspitzen*
	oncoming	*entgegenkommend*
	outline	*Umriss*
to	overbook	*überbuchen*
to	overreact	*überreagieren*
	overtired	*übermüdet*
	overwhelmed	*überwältigt*
to	pace	*schreiten*
to	pad	*trotten*
	pale	*blass*
	palm of one's hand	*Handinnenfläche*
to	pant	*keuchen, schnauben*
	parking lot	*Parkplatz*
	parking space	*Parkplatz*
	party pooper	*Spaßbremse*

past	*Vergangenheit*
to peer	*spähen*
pendant	*Anhänger*
to persuade sb.	*jdn. überreden, überzeugen*
phony	*vorgetäuscht*
to pick sb. up	*jdn. abholen*
pit	*(ugs.) Loch*
to play dumb	*sich dumm stellen*
to play innocent	*(ugs.) den/die Unschuldige/n spielen*
to play tricks on sb.	*jdm. Streiche spielen*
playful	*scherzhaft*
to plead	*flehen*
to plunge	*eintauchen*
to point sth. at sb.	*etw. auf jdn. richten*
to point to sth.	*auf etw. zeigen*
to poke	*stupsen*
to poke out of sth.	*aus etw. herausragen*
to pop up	*erscheinen*
porch	*Veranda*
practical joke	*Streich*
practically	*(hier:) so gut wie*
to press down on the accelerator	*aufs Gaspedal drücken*
to pretend	*so tun, als ob*
pretty	*(ugs.) ziemlich*
to prevent sth.	*etw. verhindern*
preview	*Vorschau*
to promise	*versprechen*
to pronounce	*aussprechen*
protective	*schützend*
to protest	*widersprechen*
to prove sth. to sb.	*jdm. etw. beweisen*
prowler	*Spanner, Eindringling, Einbrecher*
pruning shear	*Gartenschere*
to pull away	*abrücken*

to	pull the trigger	*abdrücken*
to	punch sb.	*jdn. mit der Faust schlagen*
	punctual	*pünktlich*
to	put sb. down	*schlecht von jdm. reden*
to	put sb. down	*jdn. herunterputzen*
	radiant	*strahlend*
to	reach for sth.	*nach etw. greifen*
to	reach out	*die Hand ausstrecken*
to	reason with sb.	*mit jdm. (vernünftig) reden*
	reckless	*waghalsig, unbesonnen*
	recognition	*Wiedererkennung*
to	recognize sb.	*jdn. wiedererkennen*
to	reconsider sth.	*noch einmal über etw. nachdenken*
	red-blooded	*heißblütig*
to	refuse to do sth.	*sich weigern, etw. zu tun*
to	rehearse	*vorbereiten, proben*
	relief	*Erleichterung*
	relieved	*erleichtert*
to	rest	*ruhen*
to	reveal	*enthüllen*
	revenge	*Rache, Vergeltung*
to	rip open	*aufreißen*
to	rot	*verfaulen*
	row	*Reihe*
to	rummage around	*durchstöbern*
to	run one's hand over sth.	*mit der Hand über etw. fahren*
	run-down	*heruntergekommen*
to	rush forward	*vorstürmen*
to	sacrifice oneself	*sich aufopfern*
	salmon	*Lachs*
	scattered	*verstreut*
to	scoff	*höhnisch lachen*
to	scramble through sth.	*sich durch etw. zwängen*
	scratch	*Kratzer*

to scream	schreien
to screw sb. up	(ugs.) jdn. aus der Bahn werfen
section of town	Stadtteil
to see double	doppelt sehen
to see things	Visionen haben
to seep	sickern
senior	Oberstufenschüler
to serve as sth.	als etw. dienen
shadowy outline	schattiger Umriss
shaky	zitterig, wackelig auf den Beinen
sharp	(hier:) bissig, scharf
to shatter a silence	die Stille zerreißen
She drew in her breath...	Sie atmete tief ein
She hadn't intended to...	Sie hatte nicht vor ...
She hadn't minded...	Sie hatte nichts dagegen gehabt ...
She made another wild grab for the bag.	Sie griff noch einmal wild nach der Tasche.
to shield	schützen
shimmer	Schimmer
to shiver	zittern
shoulder	(hier:) Randstreifen
to shove	schubsen
to show off	prahlen
to show oneself	sich zeigen
to shriek	kreischen
shrug	mit den Achseln zucken
to shudder	erschaudern
to shut up about sth.	etw. verschweigen
sickening	entsetzlich, ekelhaft
to sigh	seufzen
sight	Anblick
to sit up (straight)	sich aufrichten
skeptical	skeptisch, misstrauisch
skinny	dünn, mager

to	slam	*zuknallen*
to	slap	*klatschen*
to	slap a high-five	*abklatschen*
	sleeveless	*ärmellos*
to	slide	*gleiten*
	slight hitch	*kleiner Haken*
	slow motion	*Zeitlupe*
	slow number	*Schmuselied*
to	slump down	*in sich zusammensacken*
	sly	*gerissen*
	smirk	*spöttisches Grinsen*
	smugly	*selbstgefällig*
to	snap	*(hier:) fauchen*
	sneer	*spöttisches Lächeln*
to	snicker	*kichern*
to	snore	*schnarchen*
	snug	*gemütlich*
to	snuggle against sb.	*sich an jdn. schmiegen*
	So what else is new?	*(ugs.) Na, und?*
	soda	*Limonde*
	soil	*Erde*
	Sorry I'm such a downer.	*Tut mir leid, ich bin so eine Spaßbremse.*
	soundless	*klanglos, still*
	sparkly top	*glitzerndes Oberteil*
to	speed through a light	*über eine Ampel rasen*
	spine	*(hier:) Rücken*
to	splash in a puddle	*in eine Pfütze treten*
to	spoil sth.	*etw. vermasseln*
	spoiled rotten	*total verwöhnt*
to	squeak	*quietschen*
to	squeeze sb.'s hand	*jdm. die Hand fest drücken*
to	stack	*aufstapeln*
	stained	*gefleckt*
To	stall for time.	*Um Zeit zu gewinnen.*

to stammer	stottern
to stand one's ground	nicht von der Stelle
to stare	starren
to start out	herausgehen
to start toward sb.	auf jdn. losgehen
startled	überrumpelt
startling	überraschend
steady	beständig
steam of names	Aneinanderreihung von Beleidigungen
steering	Steuerung
to stick to a subject	bei einem Thema bleiben
to stick up	abstehen
stiff	steif, spießig
stoned	bekifft
stoop	Veranda
storeroom	Lagerraum
to storm out	herausstürmen
straight out	geradewegs hinaus
strand of hair	Haarsträhne
to stretch	sich strecken
to struggle to do sth.	Mühe haben, etwas zu tun
stuck	geklebt
to stuff one's face	(ugs.) sich vollstopfen
to stumble	stolpern
stunned	fassunglos
to succeed	Erfolg haben
sudden	plötzlich
suffocating	erstickend
to summon	zusammennehmen
supervisor	Leiter
surrender	Kapitulation
suspicious	(hier:) misstrauisch
to swallow sth. up	etw. verschlingen
to sway	schwanken

to swerve	einen Schlenker machen
to swing	schwingen, schwenken
to take a hint	(hier:) den Wink mit dem Zaunpfahl verstehen
to take sth. seriously	etw. ernst nehmen
Take your time.	Lass dir Zeit.
tangle of hair	Haarsträhne
tanked up	(ugs.) voll
to tease	necken
to tense	sich anspannen
terrifying	entsetzlich
That makes a lot of sense	(ironisch.) Ja, klar!
that you claimed you saw	den du gesehen haben willst
the least bit	im Geringsten
The tires spun onto the soft shoulder.	Die Reifen drehten auf dem weichen Randstreifen durch.
There's no rush.	Wir haben's nicht eilig.
There's no such thing as ghosts.	Es gibt keine Geister
They got into a playful shoving match.	Sie begannen, sich gegenseitig aus Spaß zu schubsen.
to threaten to do sth.	damit drohen, etw. zu tun
throbbing	pulsierend
to throw one's arms around sb.'s shoulder	jemandem um den Hals fallen
to throw sb. off guard	jemanden unvorbereitet treffen
to tie one's hair back	sich die Haare zusammenbinden
to tighten	fester werden
tighter	fester
till they dropped	(ugs.) bis sie nicht mehr konnten
to tilt	kippen
to toss	werfen
to trail off	verstummen
transparent	durchsichtig
to tremble	zittern, beben
to trick sb.	jdn. täuschen

to	trickle	*tropfen*
	triumphantly	*triumphierend, selbstgefällig*
	troubled	*bekümmert*
	trowel	*Schaufel*
	trunk	*Kofferraum*
to	trust sb.	*jdm. trauen*
to	try something	*(ugs.) sich daneben verhalten*
to	tug at sth.	*an etw. zupfen*
	turmoil	*Aufruhr*
	twig	*Zweig*
to	twirl	*wirbeln*
to	twist	*verdrehen*
	twisted	*gezerrt*
	uncertain	*unsicher*
to	unlock	*aufmachen*
	unreal	*irreal, unwirklich*
	unshaven	*unrasiert*
	unsteady	*schwankend*
to	urge sb. to do sth.	*jdn. drängen, etw. zu tun*
to	utter sth.	*etw. von sich geben*
	vast	*gewaltig, gigantisch*
	VCR	*Videorekorder*
to	veer	*(hier:) scharf ausscheren*
	viewing booth	*Lesekabine*
	visibly	*sichtbar*
	warehouse	*Lagerhaus*
	warmth	*Wärme*
	wary	*vorsichtig*
	was snoring away	*schnarchte vor sich hin*
	wealthy	*wohlhabend*
	weary	*erschöft, müde*
	weary	*müde, lustlos*
	What do you see in him?	*Was gefällt dir an*
	what he could have bought her	*was er ihr gekauft haben könnte*

What was the matter with him?	*Was war los mit ihm?*
whispering	*Geflüster*
wide-awake	*hellwach*
window ledge	*Fensterbank (an der Außenseite eines Gebäudes)*
windshield	*Windschutzscheibe*
wisp of cold air	*kalter Luftzug*
with a straight face	*ohne eine Miene zu verziehen*
with one motion	*mit einer einzigen Bewegung*
without further warning	*ohne weitere Warnung*
wooden crate	*Holzkiste*
to wrap around sth.	*sich um etw. wickeln*
wrecked	*(ugs.) platt, fix und fertig*
to wrinkle one's forehead	*die Stirn runzeln*
yard	*(hier:) Garten vor dem Haus*
to yawn	*gähnen*
to yell	*brüllen, rufen*
You are forgiven.	*Es sei dir verziehen.*
You're just a tease.	*Du schäkerst nur gerne.*

ÜBUNGEN

1. The Fear Street prowler

Melissa wohnt in der Fear Street und verfolgt die Nachrichten über eine Serie von Einbrüchen in ihrer Straße. Kannst du folgende englische Wörter zum Thema mit ihren deutschen Übersetzungen verbinden?

1. burglar
2. break in
3. prowler
4. steal
5. burglary

____ A. Einbruch
____ B. stehlen
____ C. einbrechen
____ D. Einbrecher
____ E. Herumtreiber

> Das Wort **prowler** bezeichnet im Englischen zunächst ganz allgemein eine zwielichtige Gestalt, die sich vor allem im Dunkeln herumtreibt und Böses im Schilde führt. Das kann ein Einbruch, ein Überfall oder aber auch Schlimmeres sein.

2. The dream car

Zu ihrem Geburtstag bekommt Melissa ein wahres Traumauto geschenkt. Unterstreiche das richtige Wort, um die Beschreibung des Autos zu vervollständigen.

Melissa's new Pontiac Firebird is tinny/shiny/flimsy and has that wonderful new car smell. Inside, it has leather/leader/tether seats and a big tearing/steering/turning wheel. Melissa gets the keys and takes it for a driven/drives/drive. When she puts her foot on the accelerator/brake/clutch, the car roars and speeds away.

3. I want it done yesterday!

In den Unterhaltungen auf Melissas Party fallen so einige umgangssprachliche Formulierungen, die im Englischen sehr oft vorkommen. Kennst du die passende Übersetzung im Deutschen?

1. So what else is new?
   - A. Bist du neu hier?
   - B. Na, und?
   - C. Ist das Teil neu?

2. He's not the most punctual person in the universe.
   - **A.** Er ist der pünktlichste Mensch, den es je gegeben hat.
   - **B.** Pünktlichkeit ist bei ihm ein Fremdwort.
   - **C.** Er ist nicht gerade der pünktlichste Mensch den die Welt gesehen hat.

3. You've got to be out of here ten minutes ago!
   - **A.** Ihr müsst alle weg hier – am besten schon vor zehn Minuten!
   - **B.** Ihr werdet in zehn Minuten gehen!
   - **C.** Vor zehn Minuten wolltet ihr alle noch gehen!

4. Another false alarm

In diesen Auszügen aus dem genervten Gespräch zwischen Melissa und ihren Eltern fehlt jeweils ein Wort. Fülle die Lücken.

1. "I told you," she said angrily. "It was too _ _ r _."
2. "And he just vanished into thin _ i _." Mrs. Dryden shook her head.
3. "You don't _ _ l _ _ _ e me, do you?" Melissa snapped.
4. "Please, Mother. Don't talk to me like I'm a _ a _ _."
5. Mr. Dryden held out his arms. "There's no _ e _ _ to be angry at us."

5. Fashion

Der Spuk erscheint nicht im weißen Laken, sondern in handelsüblicher Kleidung. Auch wird oft erwähnt, was Melissa oder Buddy anziehen. Verbinde die passenden Begriffe.

1. leather   ____ **A.** pendant
2. denim   ____ **B.** jeans
3. silver   ____ **C.** sneakers
4. sleeveless   ____ **D.** jacket
5. white   ____ **E.** t-shirt

> Denke immer daran, dass manche Dinge unterschiedlich bezeichnet werden, je nachdem, ob ein Amerikaner oder ein Brite spricht. Was würde beispielsweise ein Amerikaner zu **trainers** sagen?

6. Don't play innocent!

In Melissas Auseinandersetzung mit dem Geist fallen einige Adjektive.
Sie sind hier fett geschrieben. Kannst du ihre Gegenteile zuordnen?

1. "**Convenient**," he muttered bitterly.
2. "Stop being so **mysterious**."
3. "Don't play **innocent**." He turned his back on her
4. "You're as **alive** as I am!" she cried.

_____ A. dead
_____ B. awkward
_____ C. obvious
_____ D. guilty

7. What's a THEAD?

Es geht um Pauls Ableben. Kannst du die Anagramme dazu entziffern?

1. "I could help you find the real person who likeld _____ you."

2. "Don't you want to find out how you dide _____?"

3. Paul does not understand his thead _____.

4. He does not know how long he has been aded _____ for.

5. Melissa has no memory of linklig _____ Paul.

8. Do you believe in ghosts?

Melissa und Buddy überhalten sich über Geister und darüber, ob man daran
glauben sollte. Dabei ist es wichtig, die passenden Wörter zu kennen,
um über das Mögliche oder das Theoretische zu sprechen. Kannst du hier
die richtigen Begriffe wählen? Unterstreiche sie.

Would he laugh at her? Or would he believe/follow/trust her? It was too late
now. She had to tell him – and convert/believe/convince him.
"I knew you wouldn't believe me," she whispered.
"How can I? It's not possible/probable/profitable. It's just not possible/probable/
profitable."
"Okay," Melissa said, "I'm going to pray/pretend/prove to you that I'm telling
the truth."

9. Boyfriend and girlfriend

Buddy und Melissa sind zusammen und vor allem Buddy bringt dies auch gerne durch Körperkontakt zum Ausdruck. Hier einige Anagramme zum Thema Kuscheln und Knutschen, die du entziffern und mit der jeweiligen deutschen Übersetzung verbinden kannst.

1. GINSKIS   _____   ___ A. kuscheln

2. MACBEER   _____   ___ B. Küssen

3. LEGSGUN   _____   ___ C. rummachen

4. OAKMUTE   ___-_____   ___ D. Umarmung

10. At the library

Welcher dieser Sätze über Melissas Rechercheversuche in der Bibliothek stimmt?

TRUE / FALSE

1. The library is full of readers on that Monday morning.
2. Melissa reads through each page of every *Courier* from the last six months.
3. She does not find any stories about young people dying.
4. Melissa has to put on gloves to handle the copies of the *Courier*.

11. Can you drive me there?

Als stolze Besitzerin eines Pontiacs, kann Melissa ihre Freunde immer mitnehmen. Im folgenden Text hat man allerdings vergessen alle Wörter mitzunehmen. Vervollständige die Lücken auf der nächsten Seite mit den Wörtern aus den Kästchen.

cracking   off   picked   home

She had (1) _____ her up earlier, and now Melissa dropped Delia

(2) _____, then headed (3) _____. The late-afternoon sun was still high in the sky. The road was bubbling in the heat. Shadows from the trees she passed danced on the shiny hood. It all seemed unreal. I'm not

(4) _____ up. I'm not. The ghost is real, she told herself. Paul is real.

12. Don't spoil it!

Als Melissa und Buddy im Red Heat sind, werden einige Wörter verwendet, die zwei unterschiedliche Bedeutungen haben. Verknüpfe sie hier mit der Bedeutung, die sie im Text haben, und dann mit der zweiten möglichen Übersetzung. Wenn du dir unsicher bist, dann schlage im Wörterbuch nach.

> Wörter die du nicht kennst, kannst du ganz einfach und schnell unter **www. pons.eu** nachschlagen

1. spoil	___ A. Bann	___ I. verwöhnen
2. row	___ B. sich drehen	___ II. buchstabieren
3. mindless	___ C. geistesabwesend	___ III. sinnlos
4. spell	___ D. verderben	___ IV. rudern
5. turn	___ E. Reihe	___ V. Reihe

13. Ways of saying things

Hier sind einige Auszüge aus der brenzligen Situation, in die Melissa auf dem Parkplatz gerät. Allerdings fehlen ein paar Wörter. Fülle die Lücken.

shouted   stammered   asked   repeated   protested

1. "You–you can see him?" she _____.

2. "You really can see him?" Melissa _____.

3. "But... you're real!" Melissa _____.

4. "Let go of me!" Melissa _____.

5. "No. I wasn't," Melissa _____.

14. He's bad, man!

Pauls Kumpel Frankie, der im Supermarkt arbeitet, spricht sehr umgangssprachlich. Kannst du die Lücken in seinen Sätzen den untenstehenden Wörtern vervollständigen?

Weißt Du übrigens wofür die umgangssprachliche Kurzform „gotta" steht?

"I want to ask you about Paul."
Frankie smiled. "You really got the **(1)** _____ for Paul, huh?"
Melissa blushed. "No. That's not why... I mean... Listen, you and Paul were friends?"
"Yeah. We're **(2)** _____. Paul's a pretty **(3)** _____ _____."
"What do you mean by bad?" she asked uncomfortably, suddenly wishing she hadn't come here.
"Hey, sorry, but I gotta get back to work. If I'm late after a break, I'll be **(4)** _____."

buddies   dude   hots   busted   bad

15. An angry man

Die Aussicht auf eine Zukunft ohne Perspektive hat aus Paul einen verbitterten jungen Mann gemacht hat. Versuch einmal, diese Anagramme zu lösen, die seinen Gemütszustand beschreiben.

1. RYAGN _____   4. THENGRIDEF _____

2. RETTBI _____   5. UJOSLAE _____

3. URCLE _____

16. Ghosts don't walk

Pauls Geist kann natürlich nicht gehen, laufen und springen wie der lebendige Paul. Vielmehr gleitet, schwebt und fließt er. Wie viele englische Begriffe für gespenstische Bewegungen kannst du in diesem Wort-Spuk finden?

SPOOGLIDEGHOSDRIFTSPIRIFLOATPARANORMATERIALISELIMBHOVER

17. How did he say it?

Typisch für den englischen Sprachgebrauch ist es, nach der direkten Rede mit einem Adverb zu beschreiben, wie jemand etwas sagt. Ordne diesen Sätzen aus Pauls verhängnisvollen letzten Stunden die richtigen Adverbien zu.

1. "There are ways to get money," Paul said _____.   ___ A. politely

2. "We're just going, Officer." Paul said _____.   ___ B. bitterly

3. "Sorry," the ghost said _____.   ___ C. smugly

4. "It's where I grew up," he said _____.   ___ D. softly

18. Everyday conversation

In den letzten Kapiteln führt Melissa viele Gespräche, sowohl mit Paul, Delia und ihren Eltern als auch mit sich selbst. Verbinde die umgangssprachlichen Wörter, die sie dabei benutzt, mit den passenden Begriffen aus der Standardsprache.

1. for sure   ___ A. drunk
2. nuts   ___ B. comfortable
3. hitch   ___ C. of course
4. tanked up   ___ D. problem
5. snug   ___ E. crazy

19. Cries and shouts

Hier findest du Gruppen von gleichbedeutenden Wörtern, die der Autor einsetzt, um die letzten Kapitel abwechslungsreicher und spannender zu gestalten. Allerdings gehört ein Wort jeweils nicht in die Reihe – welches? Streiche es durch.

1. trembling – quavering – scrambling – shaking
2. dangerous – heartening – menacing – threatening
3. whispered – cried – shouted – screamed

20. Crossword puzzle

Down

1. Melissa never knows when Paul's ghost is going to appear or _____.
2. There has been a series of _____ in Shadyside.
4. The recent break-ins have all been on _____ _____.
5. Melissa is afraid of the Fear Street _____.
8. Paul's ghost has come back to _____ his killer.
9. Melissa cannot see the features of the ghost because they were hidden by _____.

Across

3. After he read about the crime wave, Melissa's father bought a _____.
6. Melissa's father thinks her _____ is playing tricks on her.
7. There have been lots of reports about the burglar in the _____.
9. Melissa's parents leave for a convention in Las _____.
10. Paul calls Melissa a _____ because he thinks she is playing games with him.

LÖSUNGEN

1. The Fear Street Prowler
1. D, 2. C, 3. E, 4. B, 5. A

2. A wild party
shiny, leather, steering, drive, accelerator

3. I want it done yesterday!
1. B, 2. C, 3. A

4. Another false alarm
1. dark, 2. air, 3. believe, 4. baby, 5. need

5. Fashion
1.D, 2. B, 3. A, 4. E, 5C

6. Don't play innocent
1.B, 2. C, 3. D, 4. A

7. What's a "thead"?
1. killed 2. died, 3. death, 4. dead, 5. killing

8. Do you believe in ghosts?
believe, convince, possible, possible, prove

9. Boyfriend and girlfriend
1.B kissing, 2. D embrace, 3. A snuggle, 4. C make out

10. At the library
1. false, 2. false, 3. true, 4. false

11. Can you drive me there?
1. picked, 2. off, 3. home, 4. cracking

12. Don't spoil it!
1.DI, 2. EIV, 3. CIII, 4. AII, 5BV

13. Ways of saying things
1. asked, 2. repeated, 3. stammered, 4. shouted, 5. protested

14. He's bad, man!
1. hots, 2. buddies, 3. bad dude, 4. busted

"gotta" ist eine Kurzform von "have got to"

15. An angry man
1. angry, 2. bitter, 3. cruel, 4. frightened, 5. jealous

16. Ghosts don't walk
SPOO**GLIDE**GHOS**DRIFT**SPIRI**FLOAT**PARANOR**MATERIALISE**LIMB**HOVER**

17. How did he say it?
1.C, 2. A, 3. D, 4. B

18. Everyday conversation
1.C, 2. E, 3. D, 4. A, 5. B

19. Cries and shouts
Diese Wörter gehören nicht in die Reihe:
1. scrambling, 2. heartening, 3. whispered

20. Crossword puzzle

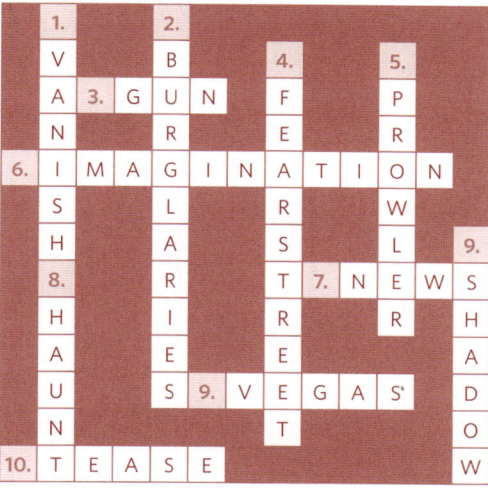

LESEVERSTÄNDNISFRAGEN

1. What has Melissa read about in the news lately and why does this make her frightened at night?
Melissa has read articles about a series of break-ins in her neighbourhood. She is frightened that the burglar – or "Fear Street Prowler" as the paper writes – will break in to her house.

2. Why did Melissa not expect to get a birthday present yet?
Melissa did not expect her birthday present because it isn't her birthday yet.

3. Why is everyone shocked when they walk into the guest room?
They are shocked to see all the presents ripped open and thrown around the room. They had all expected the presents to still be wrapped and for Melissa to open them.

4. Does Melissa's father think she is lying about what she saw in her room?
Mr Dryden does not think that Melissa is lying. Instead, he thinks that she has an over-active imagination and saw something that wasn't there.

5. Does Buddy think that Melissa is in danger?
Buddy is not worried about Melissa's safety. He thinks it is unlikely that the "prowler" will break into her home and says that she needs to relax.

6. What do Melissa's parents suggest to get her out of the house?
Mr and Mrs Dryden are going to a convention in Las Vegas and suggest that Melissa go with them.

7. What convinces Melissa that Paul really is a ghost?
When Melissa tries to grab Paul's arm, her hand goes straight through it. That is what convinces her that he really is a ghost.

8. Why does Buddy not invite Melissa into the house?
Buddy does not invite Melissa in because his house is full: both his parents and his sister already have visitors.

9. Who do Melissa and Buddy mistake for a ghost?

Sat in the lounge, Melissa and Buddy hear the footsteps of Marta, the housekeeper, and think that she could be a ghost.

10. How does Melissa start researching Paul's death?

Melissa's first step towards researching Paul's death is to go to the local library and look in newspapers from recent months for stories about young people dying.

11. What did the boy who died at South look like?

Vince, the boy who died at South, was tall, blond and is smiling in the yearbook picture.

12. Why does Melissa leave Buddy and run out of the club?

Melissa is angry at Buddy because he still refuses to believe her about Paul's ghost and does not want to talk about it anymore.

13. How does Buddy behave on the way back from the club?

Buddy does his best to forget about the argument over Melissa's paranormal experiences and talks about the club.

14. Why does Melissa drive to the supermarket?

Melissa goes to the supermarket to talk to Frankie, who is the only person apart from Paul that she recognized in the parking lot. She hopes he can tell her more about Paul.

15. Why do the police stop and talk to Melissa?

The police talk to Melissa because she is parked incorrectly – she couldn't find a space before going to see Frankie and so had parked on the street.

16. According to Melissa's theory, is Paul still alive? Why?

Melissa now has several reasons for thinking Paul is still alive: she hasn't been able to find stories about someone of his description dying; Paul's friend Frankie did not know that Paul had died; and she sees Paul without the ghost knowing about it.

17. How does the ghost try to stop Paul breaking into the house when he realises he cannot talk to him?

When ghost Paul realizes that live Paul cannot hear him, he picks up a rake and wants to use it to scare Paul away from the house: to live Paul, it would look as if the rake were moving by itself.

18. How does Melissa find Paul outside the off-licence (liquor store)?

Melissa is about to go home when she hears Paul's laugh and follows it to where he is stood.

19. Why does Melissa end up alone at home while her parents are in Las Vegas?

Melissa was going to go to Delia's house, but Delia rings to say that she will not be home until the day after. Meanwhile, Marta goes to Cincinnati for the weekend, meaning that Melissa is home alone.

20. What does Melissa take from her father's bedside drawer?

Melissa remembers that her father keeps a pistol in his bedside drawer and takes it.

21. How does Paul's ghost help to kill Paul?

Paul's ghost grabs the gun from his hand and throws it to Melissa, who then accidentally pulls the trigger.

22. Why did Paul's ghost help to kill Paul?

Paul's ghost cares about Melissa and did not want live Paul to kill her.

Notizen

Notizen

Notizen

Fear Street – gleich weiterlesen ...

PONS Fear Street
Deadly Secret – There's no escape

Kein Mensch soll erfahren, was in der nebligen Nacht in der Sackgasse geschah – darauf leisten Natalie und ihre Freunde einen Schwur. Doch dann kann einer nicht mehr schweigen und ist kurz darauf tot. Ein tragischer Unfall? Aber dann stirbt noch ein Mädchen. Natalie kann nicht glauben, dass der Mörder unter ihren Freunden ist – bis sie selbst in Lebensgefahr gerät ...

So geht Englisch-Lernen mit Gänsehautgarantie!
- Lies die spannende Horrorstory und lerne neue Vokabeln mithilfe der Übersetzungsangaben
- Mit der MP3-CD kannst du die Geschichte außerdem zu Hause oder unterwegs hören
- Unbekannte Wörter schlägst du schnell in der alphabetischen Wortliste nach

Format: 13,5 x 19,5 cm
Broschur, **128 Seiten**
ISBN: 978-3-12-010076-8

www.pons.de